To Willson, with a

C000048604

Douglas. Ma.
Maisie Mourton

LUCKY DOUG

MEMOIRS OF THE RAF
1937–1946 AND AFTER

Lucky Doug

Memoirs of the RAF
1937–1946 and After

by

Douglas Mourton

The Pentland Press Limited
Edinburgh · Cambridge · Durham · USA

© Douglas Mourton 1999

First published in 1999 by
The Pentland Press Ltd.
1 Hutton Close
South Church
Bishop Auckland
Durham

British Library Cataloguing in Publication Data.
A catalogue record for this book is available
from the British Library.

ISBN 1 85821 689 3

Typeset by George Wishart & Associates, Whitley Bay.
Printed and bound by Bookcraft (Bath) Ltd.

*To Maisie, my dear wife,
whose love and support
made this book possible.*

Preface

A<small>LL AIRCREW</small> who survived one or more operational flying tours in World War II have some unusual and, I hope, interesting tales to tell of luck, fate or chance, otherwise they would not still be here. All aircrew were volunteers.

Fifty or so years on there is a recognition that unless they are recorded now, while there is still time, they will be lost forever. Passed on at second or third hand (if at all) they probably would never be believed. Naturally, over the years, I have told my children and grandchildren many of my experiences. It is solely due to pressure from them that I am putting pen to paper, being the type that always intends to do a job of work tomorrow.

There is another reason for making this collection. It may remind future generations what their forbears endured, both civilian and fighting services, to give them some chance of leading reasonable lives. It is worth pausing now and then to consider what might have happened had the Allies lost the war. It bears thinking about.

Aircrew, by performance, lived very close together.

Squadron life was an intimate experience. We were all of the same mould, young, adventurous, living life to the full, but always conscious that many who were laughing and joking with us today would probably not be around tomorrow. In operational roles, each one was directly or indirectly dependent upon the other for survival. There was mutual trust and reliance. This promoted fondness, affection and respect. Friendships thus forged had a depth and unique quality that never existed with friendships before and for me never after. There was also a deep personal relationship between aircrew and ground crews who worked tirelessly at all hours, and outside in all weathers, to ensure that everything worked perfectly, adding to the safety of the aircrew who would fly the aircraft. In doing so they formed a close bond with the aircrew, for whom they had a deep and lasting admiration. We were as one, winning and losing together.

There were very few aircrew on Bomber Command who entered the war at the beginning, who survived to the end. Bomber Command had a higher percentage of losses than any other service of any nation. A crew's efficiency, ability and competence increased their chance of survival. But I maintain that it was 20 per cent ability and 80 per cent luck.

The air war of 1939-45 was a period of progressive change. Conditions in 1939-41 were completely different to those in the closing stages of 1944-45. The earlier years were rough, we were pioneering and we were thrown in at the deep end. Our difficulty was navigating to a target, sometimes small, in darkness, when our only means of navigating were map reading, dead reckoning and astronavigation in that order, and not many aircrew were proficient in the last. Not for us the sophisticated radar aids of later years. It was going to be a hard war. The men who survived those primitive operations of 1940 and 1941 would look back on them afterwards as almost lunatic in their crudeness compared with what came later. Aircrew, as befitted men who were statistically not long for this world, spent their last months fattened with whatever England could provide for them, unheard-of luxuries such as extra milk, sugar and real eggs and bacon.

Churchill said in September 1940, 'The fighters are our salvation but the bombers alone provide the means of victory.'

But our victory later had a hollow ring. After the war, the Government and the nation, having realised the destruction wrought by Bomber Command, rushed to distance themselves from it. Aircrews were the cream of the nation's youth, completely devoted to their task, fighting continuously for years against all odds, and it is a great travesty of military justice that we were not awarded our own campaign medal. Nor did Harris receive the peerage with which the other service commanders were honoured. Too many thought our campaign immoral, but Dr Noble Frankland, the official historian, said, 'The ultimate amorality would have been to lose the war against Hitler's Germany, one of the most vile regimes the world had ever known.'

Earlier we had enjoyed the fullest support and approval of almost every member of the population from the Prime Minister downwards. However, in the post-war years, with the country safely delivered from defeat and unspeakable tyranny, Bomber Command became the subject of much controversy. Acts of courage and high endeavour were denigrated. Much of the criticism has stuck, the critics closing their eyes to the fact that for most of the Second World War, the bombing offensive was the only strategic offensive available to the United Kingdom.

Most people have knowledge of the 'Battle of Britain' fought by Fighter Command, and Spitfire and Hurricane are familiar words. That campaign lasted only a few weeks. The campaign of Bomber Command lasted from the beginning to the end of the war, with a courage and determination rarely seen before, but with grievous losses.

The story of my time in the RAF has been compiled with the aid of my flying log book and dozens of letters which I received between 1939 and 1943, from Maisie (my wife) and my parents and various friends. I located these purely by luck in an old kitbag a few years ago. Much information has also been gleaned from the Public Records Office, Kew, where records are kept of every flight of every unit right back to when the Royal Air Force was established as a separate fighting force.

Chapter One

IT ALL BEGAN early in the year 1937 when I met Doug Richardson quite by chance. He had been a close friend of mine until about a year previously, but our ways had gone in different directions. So it was quite by chance that I met him and he told me that he had joined the Royal Air Force Volunteer Reserve.

This was an organisation that had been set up by the government to provide a pool of trained pilots, should the need arise for them, in case of war. He told me that it was very interesting, great fun, and he was having the time of his life in it. So I decided to join.

I filled in the necessary papers and in due course I received a notification to attend the Air Ministry in London for tests and a medical examination. I was intelligent and quite fit, necessary qualifications to get one of the few places that were being allotted. I duly passed these tests and also an interview with a board of RAF officers.

I was instructed to report to Woodley Airfield, near Reading, on a Monday evening at 6.00 pm. It was a small airfield, situated in the country, looking almost like a farm.

On one side, on the perimeter, were a few buildings housing the instructors' rest room, a crew room, a little canteen and some small hangars. It had a pleasant, restful atmosphere. I arrived there on an absolutely glorious evening for an aptitude test. This comprised being taken up for about thirty minutes in an aircraft and I was subjected to spins, loop the loops, slow rolls, flick rolls, in fact the whole range of aerobatics. The sensations were indescribable, like visiting a very advanced futuristic fun fair. If this was flying I knew I was going to enjoy it; I could not wait to become a pilot myself.

When we had finished the instructor asked me if I had been nervous or scared. I answered truthfully that I had not. It all seemed a wonderful experience to me. Accordingly he told me to report the following weekend, when my instruction to be a pilot would commence. That was the beginning of my career in the Royal Air Force.

We had to report every other weekend from two o'clock to around five or six o'clock on Saturday, and from nine o'clock to five o'clock on Sunday. The beauty of it was that it was not only interesting, it was well paid. We received one and sixpence an hour for all the time that we were at the airfield and a very generous allowance for travelling, which could be fiddled no end. For one thing two of us travelled down there in the same car and we both put in the claim for a separate journey. In addition we received £25 a year retaining fee, a sort of bounty. To put this in perspective, £25 in 1937 would buy quite a decent second-hand car and was more than enough to put down as deposit on a house. Cigarettes were 8d. for 20 and beer was 6d. pint.

So my training commenced. We were allowed 15 hours instruction before going solo. If you were not considered proficient after 15 hours, you were put off the course. I went solo after 12 hours.

Our instruction was on two types of aircraft, the Tiger Moth, an open cockpit biplane, and the Hawk Trainer, an open cockpit monoplane. They were both two-seaters, the seats behind each other with dual control. Our instructors were mainly ex RAF officers, a pleasant good-humoured bunch of men. My instructor often said he was reluctantly preparing us for war. We did not believe him, but how right he was.

Initially our training comprised 'circuits and bumps', the term applied to take-offs and landings. The instructor gave a running commentary and corrected any faults we were making. We were then instructed in all forms of aerobatics. Eventually we could pull an aircraft out of a spin and do a forced landing in a small field or clearing, sometimes necessary with aircraft that had only one engine which might fail. We looped-the-loop, did flick rolls, flew upside down.

The wonderful day arrived when I was told to take off on my first solo flight. Just a little apprehensive, I became airborne, did a circuit and came in to land. I realised I had muffed it, I was much too high. So I opened up, went round again and on the second attempt made a perfect landing.

And now it only remained to navigate on cross-countries. For this purpose we attended the Air Ministry in London one evening a week for navigation tuition. In due course I was sent off on my first cross-country solo flight down to Filton Airfield, near Bristol. I did the journey there quite satisfactorily, but immediately after leaving for the return journey my aircraft went into an air pocket and it dropped 50 or 100 feet and I lost my map. I had no other navigational aid. So I started to fly more or less blind back to Reading, relying on my compass course. However, I must have been slightly out, because I missed the airfield and I was lost.

Eventually I found the Great West Road and thought that if I followed this, it would take me to Reading. However, I must have passed Reading when I found it and nearly landed in the middle of London. So I turned around and retraced my flight and by now it was a cold November afternoon and beginning to get very dark. I started to panic a bit, until suddenly in the gloom I saw the airfield. I landed and saw my instructor in the middle of the airfield anxiously waiting for my return. So that was my first cross-country successfully completed.

Two more satisfactory ones followed. I was now proficient in all aerobatics, forced landings and low flying and had notched up 80 hours of solo flying. I also passed the blind flying test. This comprised flying under a hood, so simulating night flying. It necessitated flying solely on instruments – rather nerve-racking when you were unable to see what lay ahead.

Every summer we were obliged to spend two weeks on continuous training. This would represent my actual annual holiday (in industry, office staff and representatives were allowed two weeks and manual workers one week every year).

So my good friend Rodney and I decided we would

spend the two weeks camping out. We duly pitched our tent on the banks of the River Thames at Sonning, which was within easy distance of the airfield. Living conditions were primitive but very enjoyable. Each morning we dived into the river with a bar of soap and that was our hygiene finished for the rest of the day. We arrived at the airfield in time for a cup of tea and a wad (cake), and at midday we were provided with lunch in the canteen. It was cooked on the premises specially for us and was always appetising and enjoyable.

We were lucky that the weather was perfect. We flew for three or four hours daily. Every evening we went into Reading for a few drinks with some of our friends on the course, or we would try our luck with some of the local talent. We had a great advantage, as very few lads of our age were able to provide a ride in a car. Saturday night was spent at the local dance hall.

It was a good money-spinner. As no accommodation could be provided at the airfield, we were allowed to charge for either a hotel or a daily travel allowance. We chose the latter as it amounted to a higher sum. Our two weeks training eventually ended. It had been an enjoyable holiday spent in a very picturesque spot, and we were that much more proficient in our flying. And now we were to resume our usual week-end training.

On the Saturday night several of us stayed at a small pub in Reading that provided bed and breakfast. The accommodation comprised double beds so we slept with one of our mates which was quite normal in those days. We had some really hectic enjoyable evenings together. There was no corridor, the bedrooms all led one into the other, and we were often provided with entertainment. One of the fellows would sometimes bring his girl friend along to spend the night with him. After a good session of drinking, she would flit from bedroom to bedroom doing a strip-tease, accompanied by various bawdy comments Eventually we would go to bed tired and happy, though a little envious.

One weekend I returned to London on the Saturday evening after having flown during the afternoon, in order to go to a party that was being given by Reg Nutticombe, a friend of mine. He had been given the key to his sister's flat to feed the cat, and had decided that it would be a good opportunity to have a party on the Saturday evening.

I turned up there straight from Reading, about half past seven, and we found that we had a crowd of boys and not enough girls. So Reg and I went down to a cinema at Clapham Junction and Reg went to the box office and asked the girl if she would like to come to a party that evening, and whether any of the usherettes would like to come as well. After a few enquiries she came back and said that six girls would like to come but they could not be picked up until about 10 o'clock, when they finished work. My car would not hold that number, but the company I worked for garaged their vans in Brixton, where the party was being held. So at 10 o'clock Reg and I took out one of the vans, went down to Clapham Junction, picked up the girls and went back to the party.

We had had a whip round amongst the boys so on the way back we bought the drink from a pub: cheap red wine (red biddy) for the girls, decanted from a barrel into bottles, and draught beer for the boys in pails which we had taken with us. We also finished up the drink which his sister had stored away.

We danced to the popular songs of the day. These were on records played on a gramophone which needed continual winding. It was an all night affair and I carried on until about 7 o'clock in the morning, when I had to motor back to Reading for the day's flying. I realised I was not really in a fit state to fly, but when I arrived, shortly before 9 o'clock, to my horror I found I was the first one to be tested by a senior test pilot from Air Ministry to ascertain whether we were suitable to carry on to more advanced machines and night flying.

He took me up in a Hawker Hart. This had the peculiarity that the radiator had to be wound out on take-off when you were using full revs, to keep it cool. It was wound half way in on normal flying and had to be wound right in when you throttled back to land, to keep the engine warm in case you had to go around again. I forgot all these things and when we came in to land, I could hardly see the deck and he actually did the landing. I was failed. I was taken off the course. I was so disappointed and humiliated. It was about the first time that I had ever failed in something that I had tried to achieve. And so my career in the Air Force finished for the time being.

Chapter Two

IT IS STRANGE and interesting how a small incident or happening can completely alter the course of one's life. Ron Willett and I had lived opposite each other for many years and we were great friends. Although I lived now about a mile away we still met up most evenings. One Wednesday in August 1938 the weather looked pleasant so we decided we would take a walk round Wandsworth Common. If we were lucky we might meet a couple of girls. When we reached the extremity of our walk a sudden and unexpected rainstorm occurred. We ran to a nearby pub for shelter, one we had never been in before.

Having ordered a drink we realised a dance was in progress upstairs and decided to investigate. We found it was the usual formula, a three piece band comprising piano, violin and saxophone – with the girls seated at one end of the room and the boys at the other end, both ends looking each other over. It was always like that in those days.

My attention was drawn to a dark attractive girl, and I determined somehow to make her acquaintance. Ron wagered me that I would not ask her for a dance, as at that time I was very shy. She was well sought after, which made my task more difficult. However, the band announced a 'Ladies' Excuse Me Waltz', and to my surprise she approached me. I danced with her and learnt her name was Maisie Marshall and that she was manageress of a baker's shop in Clapham. I was anxious to carry things further and asked her for a date. She refused, saying she was already engaged to be married.

I forgot the incident until several weeks later when I was invited to a party. To my surprise Maisie had also been invited and I used our previous meeting to engage her in conversation. I had several dances with her and owing to my persistence she eventually agreed to meet me again. And from then on I met her fairly frequently. Her fiancé, Harry Partridge, was an inspector on the buses, and so worked on shifts.

On Christmas Eve 1938 I arranged to meet Maisie. She had worked a very long day; the shop was open from 8 am to 9 pm and being the manageress she had to cash up and take the money to a night safe at a nearby bank. So it was 9.30 pm when we left to go to the Two Brewers pub in Wandsworth, where there was a band playing and an extension until midnight.

Until she met me Maisie had been a teetotaller, but I managed to open her horizon to the delights of drinking. This particular evening she had not eaten so the drink had more effect, and there was a pleasant atmosphere amongst several of our friends. The result was that when midnight arrived she felt ill, and was obviously the worse for drink. She was afraid to go home, so we stayed in the car for a couple of hours until she felt better, obviously having been the worse for wear.

Next morning I found she had left her handbag in the car. What better excuse to call in and meet her mother, who was a widow, and her brother? It was Christmas Day and obviously they would invite me in for a drink. I drove up to her house about midday, just as a fellow was leaving it.

'Were you out with my sister last night?' he asked.

'Yes,' I replied.

'Right, come inside, I want a word with you.' I could not detect any hint of Christmas goodwill in his voice, but fortunately he was smaller than me.

But even worse was to follow. Her mother confronted Maisie and myself and was not in the best of moods. She was obviously a strict disciplinarian and a stickler for convention.

'Look here, my girl,' (my girl was twenty-two years old), 'I'm not having this. Engaged to one fellow and going out with another. It's got to stop. Make up your mind here and now, which one is it going to be?'

She looked at Maisie, and Maisie, rather crestfallen, looked at me. 'That one,' she said, glancing at me, and beginning to smile.

'Right, then tomorrow you tell Harry Partridge it's all off,' her mother ordered.

Maisie never discussed it with me, but it was obvious that she had parted company with him. I found out later that he had been very upset. By a strange coincidence Harry Partridge and Maisie's brother were evacuated from the beaches of Dunkerque in the same boat in May 1940. He confided that it had caused him great pain and anguish when Maisie had broken off her relationship with him.

Right from the beginning Maisie and I got on so well together. We both joined the Junior Imperial League (Imps) which was an organisation for young Conservatives. We took no notice of the politics, but every Friday evening there was a meeting followed at 9 pm by dancing to a gramophone. We skipped the meeting by having a drink in the nearby Sailor Prince pub, but never missed the dancing.

And we integrated with a nice bunch of friends. We had tennis evenings and organised outings to various factories and interesting places, like a Saturday night visit to witness the printing and distribution of the *News of the World*. Many Sundays we went on a hike. We would all catch a train to a nearby country station, such as Epsom Downs, quite early in the morning, and it was quite usual to cover around fifteen or twenty miles by the evening. Midday we would stop at a pub to have a drink and a bite to eat. They were happy days; we were young and high spirited, enjoying the companionship of our friends. Some bank holidays Maisie and I would go camping to Box Hill. It was not too far from London and yet it was in the heart of the country. To make things respectable we took my brother Eric, then thirteen years of age, who slept between us. But anyway we never undressed. One Sunday however my mother and father turned up unexpectedly and were quite disgusted to find that the three of us slept in the same tent. How things have altered.

The charge was 6*d*. per person per night. We took a frying pan, saucepan and kettle with us and cooked on an open fire. It was before the days of fast food and takeaways so we usually cooked respectable meals, always egg and bacon for breakfast and a reasonable midday meal. We passed the time going on long walks and swimming in a lake in a picturesque setting among shrubs and trees. And every Saturday evening there was a dance band at the nearby hotel.

We were engaged the following Easter (1939). Maisie had been promoted, having been transferred to a much larger branch and was now manageress of a big retail shop and restaurant.

One Sunday we took a ride out into the country and had tea in a restaurant. Maisie went into the toilet and washed her hands. Not long afterwards, she discovered she had left behind her engagement ring, probably because she was not yet used to wearing it. She went back into the ladies, only to find someone had taken it. It had cost £10 10s. and much to our delight we discovered all rings over £10 had a year's free insurance, so we received another one free of charge.

Eventually we were married on Christmas Day 1939, on my first leave from the RAF. She has been my minder, my mentor, my mistress – and my wife – for over fifty-nine years. More on the marriage later.

Chapter Three

IN SEPTEMBER 1939 I was working as a representative for a company selling wallpaper, paint etc. to decorators, and for the past few months there had been a reluctance to purchase goods to keep in stock owing to the threat of war; things had been very tough and I was often working from 7.00 am to 9.00 pm, catching decorators in their yards in the morning and at their houses in the evening.

When war was declared against Germany, my employment was terminated. I immediately volunteered as air crew. I wanted to get in quickly as everybody knew the war was only going to last a few months. They would not train me once again as a pilot and I settled to be a wireless operator/air gunner. Joining the RAF would be a most welcome change; it was not a patriotic gesture. No thoughts were given to the danger that might ensue.

I duly went again through all the extensive and searching tests and medical examinations and passed. I was told to report to Uxbridge at the beginning of October. In the meantime, I joined the ARP (Air Raid Precautions). It was believed that London would be subjected to massive bombing raids. The hours were

8.00 pm to 8.00 am every night, all for £3 a week. It was most boring, no bombing materialised. We spent our time in the evening just within reach of the centre, at the pub and the snooker hall, and then we passed the night playing cards, smoking and dozing. It was a most unhealthy life, and my weight dropped down to 8 stone 6 lbs.

Eventually the day arrived for me to join up. I can well remember that Maisie and my mother and father took me to Uxbridge. There was a very tearful farewell, as they did not really know when they would see their hero again.

Uxbridge was still being run more or less as a peacetime establishment. I was fitted up with all my kit, except my uniform. I was told to try on a jacket and then a tailor came along and marked it with chalk here and there to make sure it would fit me absolutely perfectly. It was the only one I ever got with which so much trouble was taken. I was issued with 'irons' (knife, fork, spoon, tin plates and mug) on which my RAF number was stamped and which would be used throughout my life as an airman, also a 'housewife' which was a needlework set for sewing on buttons, darning socks etc. The other garments comprised two pairs each of pants, socks and pyjamas, three shirts, two vests and a tie. As was the habit with most people in those days, we changed our underclothes and socks once a week. Usually our dirty clothes were collected on Monday and returned the following Friday. Sometimes the system went wrong and you had to wear the same clothes for two weeks, and often the clean clothes were returned quite damp. You would see airmen standing round the stove, steam rising from the items they were holding up.

We were treated as second-class citizens. We did all the

menial tasks like cleaning and polishing the floors and windows and we had to make the toilets really sparkle. All the time we were badgered by NCOs. The food was poor, though we were usually hungry enough to eat it all. But ever since I had packed up my civilian clothes I had been touched by the kindness and thoughtfulness of the majority of my companions, touched also by the easy, unselfconscious way in which we shared things. I had acquired that sense of 'belonging' that the uniform seemed to give all who wore it. It was as though every man who dipped his irons in the trough of the scum-ridden cold water outside the cookhouse performed, by so doing, some mystic ceremony that made him a permanent member of one large, sprawling, joke-cracking, grousing family. The company we were in enabled us to overcome the difficulties. We all had a lot in common: we were all volunteers and had a spirit of adventure, very necessary for flying in 1939. An RAF saying was, 'Only birds and fools fly, and birds don't fly at night unless they are bats,' and we knew that Uxbridge was very temporary.

The corporals in charge were typical peace-time corporals, who liked to show their authority. They would enter the barrack room in the morning at half past six: 'Stand by your beds! Come on, get out of your wanking pits! You're not on the dole now!' The majority of us had left good, well paid jobs and they probably had only joined the Air Force because they could not stand the heat in civvy street.

There was one man in our hut who appeared effeminate, and we immediately gave him the nick-name of 'Fairy'. How right we were. One morning when the corporal came in to call us he apprehended Fairy in bed with another young recruit. Especially in those days it was considered a very serious offence. Both men disappeared from our hut; we had no idea where they went. This was the only time in six years service that I encountered such a happening.

We were all confined to barracks, but two of us climbed the wall and went drinking in a local pub every evening. The following weekend I decided to go home; I had no pass but decided to take a chance. And so I arrived back to Maisie and my parents, who were completely surprised by my early return.

Chapter Four

AFTER WE HAD BEEN fitted out with our uniforms and equipment we were posted to RAF Northcotes, which was close to Grimsby. Several of us had palled up at Uxbridge. There were Wilkie, Ted Adams, Reggie Bassett, Pat Conlon, Titch Leigh and several others. Little did we know that within a few months most of them would be killed.

It was an extremely healthy life at Northcotes where we were to do our 'square bashing'. Each morning we were called at half past six and after our breakfast we did an hour's exercise, overlooking the North Sea. Then we went on ten-mile route marches, had PT, football and boxing; in fact everything was done to really fitten us up. They taught us all the drill procedures.

Northcotes was not really equipped for the numbers that were being posted there due to the start of the war. One particularly amusing thing was the fact that we had to have a bath once a week. There was a corporal in charge, who put your name in a book, not only to make sure you did not have more than one bath, but to ensure that you actually did take one. And when we all went down for this bath, we had to go three in a bath, because there were so many of us. There was Reg, myself and Ted Adams in one bath, all standing up trying to lather ourselves and rinse off. As you can guess, it was absolutely hilarious.

We had a smashing four or five weeks there and at the end I think I was fitter than I had ever been before and ever likely to be after. We had been confined to camp and our only relaxation in the evenings was a pint of beer in the Naafi. But we were always ready for bed quite early.

About May 1939 I had bought a new Morris 8 for £139. I was paying 7s.6d. a week garage which I could ill afford, and I could see that it was unlikely I would have any use for it. The price of cars had dropped dramatically owing to petrol rationing. My uncle, anxious to draw a ration on two cars, offered me £20 for my lovely Morris 8, with the provision that he would sell it back to me for the same price when the war was over, probably in a few months' time. But six years later when Germany and Japan had been defeated, there were no cars being made, second-hand cars were at a premium and my Morris 8 was now worth £300. Not being a man of honour, he broke his promise to an ex-serviceman. I never got my car back.

At the end of our stay at Northcotes the sergeant in charge raffled a bicycle and nobody dared to refuse to buy a ticket. We never heard who won it, but we learned later that the same bicycle was raffled at the end of every course.

From Northcotes we were all posted to RAF Yatesbury to be introduced to wireless operating. This was a long course stretching for six or seven months. We had to learn morse code, to be able to send and receive it at a speed of 20 words a minute. We had to master all the various signalling techniques, even semaphore and the Aldis lamp, and we had to become proficient in the theory of wireless telegraphy and the inner workings of our equipment. We were also taught how to look after pigeons; many aircraft still carried them in order to send a message, particularly an SOS if all other means failed.

It was soon after arriving here that I heard that Maisie had gone into hospital with another bout of kidney trouble, which she had suffered from for many years. She was off work for some time, but wrote me on 8 November as follows:

I am feeling almost my old self once again, and am very pleased to say that I started back at work on Monday, it was awful at first but I soon got back into it, I had a nice surprise too. They made my money up for all the time that I had been away, its the first time they have done that since I have been with the firm.

I have missed you terribly, that was why I so much wanted to go back to work so as to have something to do, I half expected you to be waiting for me when I finished, but I dare say that I shall get used to it in time, we close the shop at 6·30. now.

This illness was very worrying, the kidney being such a vital part of one's anatomy, and was to lead to a much more serious problem later on. On the other hand things were going quite well for me at Yatesbury.

Our pay was still 2 shillings a day and I augmented my wages by laying down a Crown and Anchor board. We were paid every fortnight on a Thursday morning at 11 o'clock, and we were not due on duty again until after lunch. So each time my room-mates implored me to lay my Crown and Anchor board down, and each time they lost their money, and I had made a profit of £2 or so, which was really big money when you were on 2 shillings a day.

Owing to petrol rationing, the price of cars had dropped to such a low level that I was able to buy a very good Wolseley Hornet from the company for whom I used to work, for £5. So now I organised a trip up to London every weekend, whether I had a pass or not, and I charged four passengers seven and threepence return, which was the same price as they would have paid on the railway, but they were taken door to door. As petrol was still only about one and sixpence a gallon, this showed a very good profit. I was about the only one on the camp with a car; even the Group Captain CO rode in on a bicycle every day.

The flight sergeant who was in charge of us approached me one day and said that the commanding officer would like to borrow my car for the evening. I said yes, that would be okay provided it was returned full up with petrol and I was given a weekend pass. He agreed to that. From then onwards, I loaned the car out once a week in return for a full tank of petrol and a pass.

Maisie and I still enjoyed ourselves, although separated. On 23 November she wrote:

I expect that you have well got over your night out by now and you are looking forward to the next. I'm glad that you had a real good time, you have to make the most of them these days, you must have been well tight to have danced as that is more than I can do with you. I went to a dance on Thurs and had a real good time, I didn't miss one dance, Alice introduced me to some boys from her brothers club and they were good sports, two of them took me for a drink, and although I wanted to buy a round they wouldn't hear of it. Colin turned up unexpected at about 9·30 and Alice went out with him but came back about 10·30, he is expecting to go to France any day now but doesn't seem to mind

Actually the 'phoney' war was still on; there was literally no fighting. Reports coming back from France suggested everyone was having a good time. Wine was extremely cheap and there was always the opportunity to fraternise with the local 'belles'. It was a complete change from probably going into an office every day to do a boring job.

It was early on at Yatesbury that I saw my first ENSA concert, and one of the entertainers was an unknown singer, Vera Lynn. This concert made a big impact on us – in the 1930s working class people of our age were very unsophisticated and this would have been the first time we had seen talented comedians, singers or actors in person and nobody had seen a TV. Today when I hear Dame Vera Lynn singing 'We'll meet again' and 'White Cliffs of Dover' there wells up inside me such a feeling of nostalgia that it really hurts, because with me had been all those wonderful friends, most of whom would not see 1940 out.

I had a pass most weekends but those who didn't perfected a very useful subterfuge at Yatesbury. At weekends we finished work midday on Saturday and did not resume work until Monday morning, but in general weekend passes were difficult to obtain as the Government was endeavouring to cut down travel as much as possible. In our wing there were three huts, each housing 32 airmen, which were inter-connected by a passageway at the rear which served as an entrance to the communal ablutions.

The only time anyone would be noticed as missing would be at 'Lights out' on Saturday night. The procedure was that an officer and NCO would enter the first hut, the NCO would shout, 'Stand by your beds,' and the officer would proceed up one side and down the other, making sure every bed was occupied. Then 'Goodnight, men,' 'Goodnight, sir,' the NCO would turn the lights out and they would proceed to the next hut by the front entrance. Then the action took place. There would be a rush of men through the rear passageway to the second hut. They would be either men who had filled in for an absentee in the first hut and were now returning to their own bed, or men from the first hut who were filling in for absentees in the second hut. Then after the officer left the second hut there would be a scramble to the third hut. Sometimes as many as eight would be absent without leave. It happened every weekend, but no officer ever noticed he was passing the same face twice. The going price for filling in for an absentee was two cigarettes.

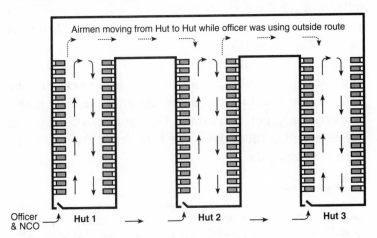

To those who stayed behind, Sunday morning breakfast was a luxury. It was one hour later than usual, and two volunteers would proceed to the cookhouse to fetch thirty-two real eggs and thirty-two rashers of bacon back to the hut, and there would be 'seconds' for one or two lucky ones because of the absentees. The newspaper man would have been round, and one could lie in bed as late as one wished. I did not however see many Sunday mornings at Yatesbury. But food rationing came into full force at the end of 1939, and eggs and bacon became just a memory.

Some of us lads went into town one Saturday afternoon for a change, and it was then, around about the end of November, that I decided it would be a good thing to get married. So I phoned Maisie up at the shop where she was working and told her that I was being granted a pass for the Christmas holidays and would she like to get married then. She said something about asking her mum, but eventually agreed and she arranged for the banns to be called out for three weeks running, as was necessary. This made the earliest day we could get married Christmas Day, 25 December 1939.

This was particularly satisfactory to Maisie as she was due back to her full time job on 27 December, and she figured she would need a day's rest after our first night. Workers only got Christmas Day and Boxing Day as holidays, and in those days even New Year's Day was still a normal working day.

Dear Doug,

I saw your people yesterday and told them the news, they were rather surprised but didn't seem to mind, Mum went today and put the banns up for me, we can be married at 1-30 Xmas day at the church at the top of the turning next to mine, I would like it to be there if its O.K. with you, if we were married on Boxing Day it would mean that I would have to go to work stright away the next day, I would rather spend the day after with you.

Your mother & father are going to see about your banns, I will write as soon as I know, also I have asked Gladys to be bridesmaid & she said that she would.

However, shortly afterwards, Gladys, my cousin, decided to get married to Ray, who was in the RAF Volunteer Reserve, training as an observer (later renamed 'navigator'). We had all been very friendly and I can well remember that on the day war was declared, I gave him a lift to Mitcham to report to the reception centre there to enlist in the regular RAF. On the way back the air raid warning sounded; it caused real panic. Pedestrians were running for shelter, most traffic stopped and the drivers and passengers took cover. I carried on; I had not far to go, but my legs were trembling. When I arrived back home, I found my mother, father, uncle and aunt down in the cellar, gas masks on, only taking them off to have another slug of whisky. Actually, it all turned out to be a false alarm.

Ray, the fiancé of Gladys, wrote to me on 5 December as follows:

> I have now been here a month, and am billeted at the above address with two fellows who were in the same section in London prior to the War. One of them has succeeded in making "friends" with the wife, a naval officer at sea, and therefore we see little of him. Apparently her cooking is superb and he has not yet fully sampled all the dishes which she can serve, although I understand that the hors d'oeuvres + sweets are usually the same.
>
> During the weekend, I had leave, & visited my fiancée. During my stay at your London residence, I learned from your charming "wife" of the pomp + ceremony with which you intend to celebrate your Xmas

leave, and I should like to take this opportu- of congratulating you. At present, it seems unlikely that I shall have the pleasure of attending your triumphant march between an arch of loop aerials to the tune of testing signals from a hundred buzzers. If I can however, perhaps you will not object if we arrange a double celebration, and I shall be glad if you will let me know.

Maisie wrote to me on 16 December:

I have been dashing here and there all the week getting things settled, but now everything is arranged.

There will be one saloon car to take us which holds six persons and will do three runs for 21 shillings. With your father's and uncle's cars that should be sufficient.

I have ordered trestles and forms, they look very nice when laid out, and my mother and yours are seeing to the food between them, and the cake is on order. And we can have the organ after all.

Would you mind if I went and bought my wedding ring? Please let me know soon, as it mustn't be forgotten.

Would you let me know how many boys you will be bringing for catering purposes, but there won't be any accommodation. [I suggested a round bed, but it did not meet with approval.]

It doesn't seem possible that in ten days we will be married, and I'm glad we decided as we did.

Will write again soon,

All my love,

Maisie.

26

So it was decided we would have a double wedding with Gladys and Ray. It was a bitter cold, snowy December day when we got married. We could not afford to go on a honeymoon and we stayed at my parents' home for the week after the wedding. On the wedding evening we had a great party; many relations attended and Maisie and I did not retire until about 2 am. But that still left enough time to carry out the marital duties quite successfully.

Shortly afterwards Ray finished his training as observer and was promoted to sergeant, but he was killed on one of the first raids he took part in. Although I would be doing the same job in a few months' time, it never occurred to me that I might share the same fate. I just didn't think about it.

Now, being married, I had to make an allowance to my wife, so my pay was actually reduced to 6 shillings a week as there was a further deduction made for barrack room damages and so on. Beer was 6d. a pint, cigarettes 1s. for twenty. But with the Crown and Anchor board, hiring out my car and playing cards I was relatively wealthy. In fact I regularly paid a friend two cigarettes to polish my bed space, while I relaxed on the bed.

On 30 December I wrote to Maisie:

I had a good journey back to camp, and the changeover hasn't been as tough as I expected.

I had the most enjoyable week of my life and I feel happy and contented and I think that is why I don't feel too bad down here as I can always think about it and realise how lucky I have been. I hope you feel the same way about it, because although you must miss me a lot as I miss you, the memories of a happy week certainly eases it a great deal.

ROYAL AIR FORCE.

FORM 859.

CLAIM TO FAMILY ALLOWANCE in respect of a RECRUIT,
A RESERVIST,¹ or a SERVING AIRMAN.

Name in full	DOUGLAS ROBERT MORTON	Official No.	904638
Date of Birth :	10.5.16	Particulars of Marriage :—	Date 25th December 1939
			Place Wandsworth
Date of Attestation :	11.10.39	Rank AC2	Unit RAF Uxbridge

If the Airman has previously served in His Majesty's Forces (a) Previous Unit .... (b) Date of Discharge............

* Need not be filled up for a Reservist joining on Mobilisation.

DECLARATION BY THE AIRMAN.

Questions 1 to 5 must be answered in the Airman's own handwriting.

WARNING.—Any false statement knowingly made in filling up this form will render the person making it liable to prosecution and refusal of all allowances.

1. State whether " Married," or " Widower,"** or ' Separated from Wife "**   Married

2. Particulars of person to whom family allowance is to be paid :—
   - a. Full Christian Names and Surname   Kathleen May Morton
   - b. Address   41, St. ?, Earlsfield, London SW18
   - c. Nearest Post Office   Earlsfield P.O.
   - d. State whether " Wife " or " Guardian of Children "   Wife

3. Particulars of children† for whom family allowance is claimed by me who are under the age of 14 and are still living, and are the legitimate children of myself or my wife, children born to myself and my wife before our marriage, or children adopted under the provisions of the Adoption of Children Act, 1926

TO BE FILLED UP IN THE CASE OF A SERVING AIRMAN.

This form was received by me on (Date)   25.1.40
with the declaration duly completed.

(a) The Airman's substantive pay being .... 2/- .... per diem;
.... per diem has been noted for deduction on account of allotment.

(b) The following certificates‡ in support of the Airman's claim are attached
...... Marriage Certificate

.... Accountant Office

Date   25.1/40   .... Unit.

4. Is any allowance or pension being issued to your wife or for any children, step-children or adopted children in respect of any person or persons who have served in the Royal Navy, Army or Royal Air Force.
   ...(Answer " Yes " or " No ")
   If so, state :—

Service No.	Rank.	Name.	Regiment or Unit.	Amount of Pension or Allowance.	Cause of issue.

5. (a) (i.) Are you living with your wife ?   YES
   (ii.) If not, explain in what circumstances you are living apart
   (b) If separated from your wife, state :—
   (i.) What allowance you are making to her
   (ii.) Whether such allowance is paid voluntarily or under an Order of Court

†† I declare that the foregoing particulars are correct and I claim Family Allowance for my wife and family.

28

And on 1 January Maisie wrote to me:

After you left me on Friday I felt awfully down in the dumps and fed up about you going back, but once I had got to work I realised how lucky I was to have had such a happy week and I became quite contented. But I did miss you and often lie awake for a while and think about you and how much I love you.

Early in the New Year back at Yatesbury, the weather turned bitterly cold; in fact it was the lowest temperature ever recorded on Salisbury Plain. There were heavy falls of snow and this brought down power cables and telephone lines. We were completely cut off from the outside world and the emergency generator provided light but no heat.

Our diet consisted of a meat pie a day provided by a local factory, and a cup of cocoa morning and afternoon made from melted snow. Lessons were cancelled, and the only way we could keep warm was by organising slides on the ice-covered football pitches or running round them.

Each evening a few of us trudged three miles through the snow to the nearest pub. Here we could get a slice of bread and cheese, there was a roaring fire, and after a couple of pints we felt really good. Then came the very demanding three miles back and through the barbed wire to our hut. This was much quicker than going through the guard room.

After a few days the camp was hit by a virus epidemic. The Medical Officer decreed that all windows must remain open day and night, and because of the black-out, dark blue bulbs were fitted to all electric lights. Now we could not even read and because of the intensive cold we went to bed early, fully clothed under our allotted three blankets. I remember one night our whole hut (thirty-two men) was hit by the virus, giving us all acute diarrhoea. Three toilets were completely inadequate; some were sitting on wash basins, others crouching in the roadway, and all in complete darkness. There was a great deal of clearing up to do next day.

Some days later we were all assembled in our various wings (there were several thousand airmen at Yatesbury) and told we were getting a week's leave. Almost immediately afterwards this was cancelled, as owing to further heavy falls of snow railway trains could get no further than Reading (about 40 miles due east) from London and there was little road transport. Our passes were cancelled and we were forbidden to leave the camp. But it was still early morning and Wilkie and I decided we would break camp and try our luck at getting home. Wilkie had been my best man at our wedding.

We cut across the playing field, then by a roundabout route to the main road, the only way to avoid being apprehended. A series of long walks and short lifts brought us to Reading. We got a train to London, then by underground to my home by about 9.00 pm, in time for a much needed meal, then to the local for a few pints. Wilkie stayed the night with us and went home next morning.

Then followed several days of blissful warmth and rest and the companionship and more with Maisie. Eventually the weather improved. I met up with Wilkie in London and we returned to Yatesbury. We found out that apparently our break-out had caused several hundred others to follow suit and we were all put on a charge of being absent without leave. We were wheeled in front of the CO, ten at a time, our punishment being two days' loss of pay. Well worth it.

During this period Maisie continued with her work as manageress of a baker's and restaurant. She was well paid but was compelled to work such long hours as would seem unbelievable today. It was six days a week, from 8 am to 6.30 pm, Friday and Saturday till 9 pm. And being manageress, there was cashing up to do after the shop closed and then depositing the day's takings in a night safe at the local bank.

I had many real good friends at Yatesbury, men who would share their last cigarette with you, lend you their last shilling if it was necessary. None of us seemed to take much interest in the way the war was progressing, possibly because we were still in the period of the 'phoney war'. The general feeling was that the war would not last very long; unfortunately this was true for the majority who shared my hut. The general public also thought it would be a short war. In January 1940, my uncle Linton who worked in the Chatham Dockyard wrote:

> Somehow I don't think it will develop into a war on a huge scale, I'd like to see it finished before the summer comes and get back to normal.

One weekend Maisie and I stayed at the home of Ted Adams who slept two beds away from me. He was married with three children and owned a garage with his brother. He was thirty years old and had volunteered on the outbreak of war. Although there was not a great difference in our ages, thirty to us seemed a long way off and we looked upon him as rather an old man. He lived in a small village on Salisbury Plain and, on one occasion, Maisie and I spent a very pleasant week-end there. His wife made us very welcome; they were good company. I always got on well with children, playing games and telling them stories I made up.

I was very upset to learn after the war that Ted had been killed, particularly so because it happened on 21 March 1945, only a few weeks before the war ended. Apparently he was flying in a B25 Mitchell which was destroyed by flak over Bockholt, and all five crew were killed. He was buried at Bockholt but later reburied at Reichwald British Cemetery in a collective grave. His rank at that time was Warrant Officer. I have no doubt he would have been offered a commission on more than one occasion, but knowing him as I did, he preferred the life in the Sergeants' Mess. I can well imagine the distress of his wife and children. The war being almost over they would have been eagerly awaiting his return.

Another weekend we spent with Wilkie, staying at a nearby hotel. It was during this weekend that I realised how thin and unwell Maisie looked. In the morning she stood on a chair to pull the curtains and I saw the outline of her figure. She had had many serious illnesses as a child with several operations to remove stones from her kidney. She now weighed only 6 stone 10 lbs. Something drastic needed to be done.

It was shortly after this that the trouble was diagnosed. One kidney had failed and needed urgently to be removed. Maisie went into hospital and her kidney was taken out, this being a really serious, major operation in 1940, even experimental. The first information I had about this, in early April, was from my father, in a very matter of fact letter:

Dear Doug,
Hoping you are keeping fit and well. Maisie has to undergo an operation on Friday to have her kidney out. If you can get along on Saturday, they will let you in.

Almost like having a tooth out.

I also heard the news from her mother as follows:

my Dear Doug.
Maisie asked me to drop you a line to Say she went into Hospital quite Contented, They gave her a nice dinner she had a Bath + was nice + Comfortable in Bed where I left at 2.15, I could not stay as the Doctors were coming round the ward.
she is in Bed 29.
Elizabeth Ward
St Thomas's Hospital
+ Visiting days are Sun from 2. till .3.30 + Wed. 2.30 to 3.30 only two Visitors at Bedside at one time. I have written you el this as I know she will be pleased to hear from you. I shall go Wed. to see her + will write you after, if she is not allowed too. I hope you had a safe return

*on Sunday + ko trouble the other end
I rang up your mum & Dad told them
maisie went alright Etc.
So Cherio Doug all the Best-
hoping Maisie will soon be fit again
love Mum Marshall*

The entry into hospital must have been very sudden as I had been home the previous week-end.

Reading through the letters I received from Maisie up till this operation, never once did she complain. She never mentioned the problems she was having, or the pain that later I discovered she had been suffering. Obviously she did not want me to worry, but to keep these things to herself showed the strength of character she possessed and still possesses. Incidentally, after over fifty-nine years since the operation she has never had any ill-effects and is in very good health.

In May, after some weeks in hospital, she went to a convalescent home in Swanley, Kent to recuperate. I visited her as often as possible, but one particular weekend stands out. On the Saturday night I was on guard duty, finishing at 6.00 am. I started at once on the big hitch-hike, eighty or ninety miles to London, across London, and then about another twenty miles to Swanley. It went well and I arrived about lunchtime. My car was out of action and Wilkie was trying to fix it over the week-end.

In the afternoon we went for a walk down into the valley and up the other side. We lay in the grass and as so often before, the inevitable happened – we made love. When we got up to return, to our embarrassment we realised we had performed in full view of the convalescent home, which was not far away on the other side of the valley.

I started back to camp about 5.00 pm. It went well until I got to Marlborough about 9.00 pm. I had met a fellow airman on the way and we entered a pub. It had been a long day and I had quite a few drinks. When we continued our journey it was pitch dark. There were no passing cars and we had to do the long journey on foot. Then through the barbed wire into my hut. I was completely knackered, and had the prospect of only an hour or two of sleep.

I received a letter from Maisie shortly afterwards.

My Darling.

Sunday was one of the best days that I have spent for a long time, it was so lovely to be with you again and after the first two or three minutes it seemed as though we had never been parted, actually I would have prefered to say good-bye to you alone but the time went so quickly that I thought, to come to Sidcup with you would give us longer together; as time goes on I find myself loving you more, and wishing for this wretched war to end so that we can be together at all times.

Her recuperation at the convalescent home having finished, Maisie wrote on 25 May:

Everything is OK for me to come home on Sunday. My side hasn't healed up yet, so I will have to go to the hospital three times a week, but I won't mind as long as I am home. I have gained 13 lbs since being here and they are very pleased with me.

So things were going well, and in due course Maisie returned home as arranged.

Chapter Five

WE DECIDED THAT it would be nice to start living together in rooms. Now that we were married it was comparatively easy to get a permanent sleeping-out pass, so I went around making enquiries until eventually I found two rooms that we could have. I immediately got on the phone to Maisie and told her to come down as soon as she could manage it. A day was eventually agreed when I would meet her outside the main gates and she would be on the coach from London. She duly arrived. For some reason I was late in coming to meet her, and she had to put up with hundreds of Air Force fellows coming out of the main gate, giving her the come-on and various wolf whistles until I eventually arrived.

We went along to the address where I had arranged the accommodation, but unfortunately the lady had had some Land Army girls billeted on her a couple of days previously and she could not accommodate us, so we were stranded. We walked and walked, making enquiries here, there and everywhere, until it got to about 9 o'clock in the evening and I put Maisie into a pub with a drink while I carried on searching. Eventually, about 10 o'clock, I came to a farm house owned by a Mr Smart. I asked him if he could possibly accommodate us. He said no, they had never done anything like that before, but after some pressure from me he agreed that we could stay there for the night. I went back and collected Maisie, took her to the farm, and in actual fact we stayed on there indefinitely. We got on very well with Mr and Mrs Smart. She was an old lady, a bit of an invalid, but he was quite an active old boy, farming in the old traditional way. The farm was situated in Compton Bassett, a lovely part of Wiltshire and only a few miles from the camp.

He had three teenage daughters at home and he loved me to bring several of the Air Force fellows down for the evening, when we would stand around the piano while one of the daughters played, singing at the top of our voices and drinking pints of his home made cider.

We helped with the hay making. This was the old method where it was cut with a scythe, collected in carts, and piled up to make a very presentable haystack.

At the end of the first week I asked him how much he wanted for our board and lodging. He said, 'Well, I don't know – I've never done this sort of thing before,' and it was left and left, until we had been there about four weeks. I then insisted that we had to pay something and he suggested a pound a week.

Mr Smart had a spaniel bitch, and she had about five puppies. Dogs in those days existed on the scraps and bones left from the table, obviously not enough for a mother who had a family to feed, so every day she would leave her puppies and wander off, usually returning with a rabbit she had caught. This she would share with the puppies; nothing was left, not even the head and fur.

Maisie and I had a very happy time there. We went home for the occasional weekend to see our parents and gradually the spring turned into early summer. It was a very nice summer, that summer of 1940. Around about June we went home for the weekend and when I returned on the Monday morning I found that the entire course that I was on had been posted, to be trained as air gunners on squadrons, because there was a crisis: France was being overrun. As the German armies swept across France, and Britain entered her season of unbroken disaster, half-trained crews were sent to squadrons.

The tragic thing was that the majority of those who had been posted from my course did not last more than three or four months. They had been given a quick training as air gunners on various squadrons and then sent out on daylight raids on Blenheims. This was an aircraft that was suicidally ill-fitted for its role of a daylight tactical bomber. Cruising at 180 m.p.h. the Blenheim was almost 200 m.p.h. slower than the fighters it would meet. Lightly armed, its only chance of survival was to find cloud or attempt a hedge-level escape. The bad news began to filter back in various letters I received.

From Maisie on 16 September 1940:

I have some bad news to tell you. Remember my cousin Bert who was at Yatesbury with you, well he was killed last week at Lincoln. Their plane was badly damaged after a raid on Germany and crashed, all four of the crew were killed. He was an only child. My aunt was terribly upset and went to Lincoln where he was buried.

Then Eddie Abery went; he had slept in the next bed to me at Yatesbury. I wrote a letter of condolence to his mother and received the following reply:

103 Station Rd
Forest Gate
London E.7.
8/8/40

Dear Douglas,

We are writing to express to you our appreciation of your kind letter to us in our great sorrow.

But we never had the pleasure of meeting you. Eddie often spoke of you to us but hope to do so when you can spare a little time from one of your very short leaves

It is a great consolation to us to know our dear boy was thought so much of by his Friends in the service, and think you summed it up exactly, when you say, he was a grand Pal, he was just as popular at his school & his work, and we have suffered an irreparable loss of a very lovable lad, how proud of him we were is beyond us to say, now we have only a memory to keep within us, Sacred.

Could you give us Reggie's address as we received a Floral tribute from him & his mother, but, we are unable to thank them as we have not their address, so could we trouble you to forward it on, either his service address or his home will do, we do not even know his other name only Reggie.

the Paper, on which a description of his Funeral etc were published, and that will tell you more than we can.

Again thanking you for your kind thought for us, and all best wishes for your future, also for your Wife's Sympathy. please convey our thanks to her. and trust we shall hear from you

Yours Very Sincerely

E and E Abery.

She would have received a telegram initially like the one on page 42 and this would be followed by a letter from the Squadron Commander. The importance of the contribution made by the missing airmen to both the efficiency of the squadron and its social life was well made in these letters, and they followed a standard format as follows:

Dear
It is with the very deepest feeling of sorrow that I have to confirm my telegram telling you that your son
                failed to return from the raid on
          on the night of   I am afraid that
there is absolutely no information I can give you as no signal was received after the aircraft took off, and none of the other crews operating that night had anything to report.
    It is quite possible, of course, that he and the other members of the crew landed safely on enemy territory, and

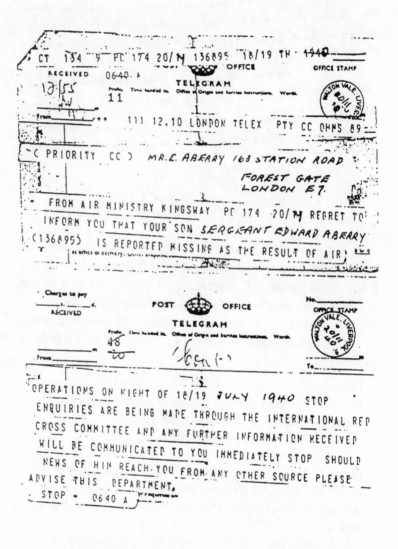

The message that every airman's parents dreaded.

are now prisoners of war, which we sincerely hope is the case, but nothing definite is known at the moment. You may be assured that I will let you know at once should any news come through. If you hear anything before we do as sometimes happens, we should be very grateful if you would let us know at once.

Your son's going has left a bad gap, not only in the work of the Squadron, where his enthusiasm for his work made him one of our most capable Wireless Operators, but also in the Sergeants' Mess, where he had found many good friends. We all realise that nothing we can say can do anything to relieve the grief and anxiety this news must cause you, but we should like you to know that we share these feelings. I trust that you will accept this letter as a sincere expression of the sympathy we all feel for you in your loss and the grief we share.

If there is anything I can do to help, I trust that you will let me know without hesitation. I feel that you might like to know the names of those who were with your son on the night in question, and enclose a list giving their names and next of kin.

Yours sincerely,

After a bad day for missing aircraft the Squadron Commander could well have over twenty letters to send to parents. The telegrams and the letters sent out would be read and re-read by the family, seeking some sign for hope. They would probably be passed from generation to generation.

But the family would continue to hope that their son had baled out and become a prisoner-of-war. In 15 per cent of the cases this would happen. The other 85 per cent would receive eventually a letter from the King:

BUCKINGHAM PALACE

The Queen and I offer you
our heartfelt sympathy in your
great sorrow.

We pray that your country's
gratitude for a life so nobly
given in its service may bring
you some measure of consolation.

George R.I

Mrs E AGERY

And then I received the following letter from my best friend of all at Yatesbury, Reggie Bassett:

sgts mess,
R.A.F.
West Rayaham.
Norfolk.
15/8/40.

Dear Doug,
I was immensely glad to have your letter as I was beginning to despair of hearing from you. Now for some real gen.*

We have had no further medical since Yatesbury, and had three weeks training only before being posted to 18 Squadron, and the next day we were on an operational trip. Since that time I have been over five times, three trips being successful but on the other two we had to return owing to absence of cloud cover — all our trips being daylight ones. Also I have stood by for many more but did not take off.

During the last four
weeks we have lost seven
* kites and included in these
are four blokes who came
with us from Yatesbury —
Hatch, Gibson, Barrett and
Land. Then, of course, there
was Eddie who was killed

If I were you I would
definitely turn down the
job but, personally, I find
it very exciting.

Have encountered a 109
and a seaplane and A.A.
fire with no detrimental
results and have caused
some damage to at least
three dromes.

I am pleased that Maisie
is well and between you
and me, her worries are
well founded, so give the
matter your earnest and
unselfish consideration.

This camp is quite good
although it is well out in
the wilds. There is
positively no bullshit and

we get out quite a bit.
Norwich is farthest away
— about 30 miles — but we
hire a taxi and creep in
there very often.
I am concentrating on
lasting until Sept 14th *
next, when I get twelve
days leave, so wish me
luck.

I wonder if it would
be possible for you to
arrange something then
for I would dearly like
to see you again.
The 'boys' send their
regards to yourself and Dave
— please don't lose
touch with me!
All my very best
wishes.
Sincerely,
Reg.

---

*Gen – RAF slang for information. Kites – RAF slang for aircraft.
Note: The loss of seven aircraft referred to would have been out of a squadron strength of about twelve aircraft. Replacement crews and aircraft would be continually necessary.

I replied to this letter, but he wrote again on 14 September:

Thanks very much for your letter. I am getting quite an experienced hand now and have added many hours operational flying time to my log. Was due for leave this Saturday, but since last week we have been confined to camp and leave has been stopped because there is some flap on. It seems our meeting will have to be deferred.

Aircrew went home on leave every six weeks, as operational flying was traumatic and a great strain on the nerves and body. When their leave was up, they would say good-bye looking fit and well, and it would have required a positive effort by their families to imagine them coming to any harm in the six weeks before their next leave was due. When bad news did arrive it was a severe shock, even more so if it arrived a day or so after they had left.

I never did meet up with Reg and he never got the leave he was looking forward to so much, as shortly after I heard he had been killed.

On hearing the news Maisie wrote: 'I felt very sorry indeed to hear about poor old Reggie, and know just how you feel. It seems that all the best people are being taken, he always was unlucky.'

Later I heard that Du Plessis, a South African, had been killed on a daylight raid off Norway, and Pat Conlon, a very religious type, had been shot down and drowned after attacking German shipping off Holland. All were good friends from Uxbridge, then North Coates, and then Yatesbury. What an amazing piece of luck it had been for me. I just happened to be on a weekend pass when my course had all been posted to operational squadrons engaged on daylight bombing missions, the most dangerous of all. While all my old friends had been coping with so much trauma I had been enjoying life in a lovely environment with my wife, during a summer that had been particularly fine. But I knew that shortly my turn would come to take part in raids on Germany.

I finally passed out as a wireless operator at the beginning of August 1940 and was posted to the air gunnery school at Stormy Down, near Porthcawl in Wales, so Maisie returned home.

Soon afterwards I received a letter from her:

> I have found myself a job, it's in that tobacconist at the top of our road. They offer me 30/- a week, with Tuesday off and every other Sunday. If you don't want me to take it, I won't.

But I did.

We received a nice letter from Mr Smart, the farmer with whom we had lived at Compton Bassett:

> Pleased to receive your letter and to hear you passed your Exam, it is a credit to you which we all feel proud, as you are one of the family and your wife, if ever you are this way do call and see us there is always a bed and food but no cider now but will get the old barrel charged again. Should like a night like we had before, what-a-to-do.

This was the night before we said goodbye, very typical of the wonderful relationships that were forged during the war.

Chapter Six

I SPENT AUGUST at the air gunnery school. The weather was glorious, as it was throughout the summer of 1940. We were under canvas and were situated two miles from Porthcawl. We went down therefore most evenings to have a beer or two and we passed through a farm where we could get a poached egg on toast and a glass of milk. Looking back, it now seems impossible that a real egg in those days was looked upon as a luxury.

Our course consisted of lectures on the Browning machine gun, air firing at drogues, although in actual fact we only spent 13 hours flying during the whole of the course. In spite of the frequent news we received of losses in Bomber Command there was still no apprehension on the part of anyone. Our turn would come, but it still seemed a long way off. I never knew of anyone dropping out, although it was still possible.

I passed out at the end of August 1940 as 'an average air gunner' now entitled to wear the coveted Air Gunners' brevet and we were promoted to sergeant at the rate of seven and ninepence a day, which was a big increase on what we had been receiving. The flying brevet was much

sought after. It signified to everyone that you were part of
the air crew of Bomber Command, and as such you were
an instant hero wherever you went. In fact the Air
Gunners' brevet could be purchased in tailors' shops
which sold uniforms. I knew several airmen who bought
them, and easily affixed them on their uniform while on
the train going on leave. On arriving home they would
receive the adulation of their friends and neighbours, and
possible a few free drinks. On the return journey they
would take them off and revert to their normal status.

We then moved on to Abingdon for the final part of our
training. Abingdon was an OTU, that is an Operational
Training Unit, where we would fly on the aircraft of the
squadrons to which we were going to be attached.
Abingdon was a very solid peace-time station. The
quarters were comfortable, the food was good.

The initial part of this OTU course consisted of
learning to fly in a Whitley bomber and to operate its
many systems and procedures. The main part of the
course consisted of long range cross-country exercises, air-
to-air firing, and learning to play one's part as one of a
team.

The peculiar part is that still nobody seemed to take
much interest in the way the war was progressing, and we
did not seem to realise at this stage, in August/September
1940, that England was on the brink of defeat. However
we had a rude awakening when we were all put on guard
duty one night. Every tenth man had a rifle. The other
nine had pick handles. This showed the state of
unpreparedness we were in at this time. A few paratroops
only would have been needed to take the airfield and

*Sgt. Douglas Mourton having passed
as a wireless operator/air gunner, 1940.*

Maisie Mourton, 1940.

buildings. In the evening the church bells started ringing, which was the signal that an invasion had commenced. This really started the adrenalin running. It made you a bit wobbly at the knees, but as it turned out it was a false alarm. This would have been the flap that Reggie Bassett referred to in his last letter to me on 14 September (see page 48).

After about a week we were transferred to Stanton Harcourt, which was another airfield, classified as a satellite of Abingdon. This had been hastily constructed. There were very few buildings, and once again we were under canvas, but the weather was still marvellous. We did a lot of flying here, especially at night when we were sent off on quite long cross-country journeys in order to familiarise ourselves with the aircraft, and to try and give us some of the conditions under which we would be flying over Germany.

Later we flew quite often on triangular courses over the North Sea, lasting six to eight hours. Initially we were with instructors, but later on we flew without them. Very occasionally an aircraft would go missing, owing to the crew flying on a reciprocal course in error. They could be seen on radar flying farther away from England. One can imagine the crew anxiously waiting to hit the coast, until they finally ran out of petrol.

On our spare evenings we hitch-hiked into any of the big towns round about, for whist drives, dances or any other thing that would entertain us. Once again I made some marvellous friends here.

Eventually our training finished. We were now fully fledged air crew and we were sent off on fifteen days leave before joining our squadron. Life was still very pleasant indeed.

But in London it was a very different story. The population were enduring hardship and danger that had never been experienced before. Night after night Germany projected massive attacks on the capital. Having aircraft based in France, their bombers could make two or three raids a night, whereas our flights took eight hours or longer. Goering had failed to destroy Fighter Command and achieve complete supremacy in the air, owing to the heroic defence by our fighter pilots. This had been a necessary prelude to the invasion of England, which Hitler now put on the back-burner. Instead his plan was to bomb England into submission.

In September, Maisie wrote to me:

Here things seem to be getting worse, where will it all end? Uncle Jack came over today, he is very worried about his mother, as they had a bomb drop opposite their house and she has taken it very badly, it seems so wicked old people have to suffer too, she is ninety on Tuesday.

We have been very busy lately, people buying sweets for the air-raid shelters. They start lining up to get them about 5 o'clock, I am told they are getting very crowded and they stay in them till about 7 o'clock in the morning.

My mother wrote on 17 September:

Things are very uncomfortable here at present, but we are getting used to it, but they don't give us five minutes peace. Beat's [my aunt] house was bombed and they have come to live with us. There is 14 of us sleeping in the cellar, including the cat. We haven't had any gas since last Sunday.

Poor old Eric [my brother] has to run home quick from work every evening about 7 o'clock and then we are in the cellar until breakfast time.

The cellar had only been used for storing coal; it was dirty without any lighting. Imagine spending night after night there for nearly twelve hours. I wonder what the toilet arrangements were.

Maisie wrote on 18 September:

Your Grandmother had a time bomb dropped near her house and they all had to evacuate and are now staying with your Mum, what a life. We visited your Mum for tea. The siren went so we had to stay. Mum and Stan and I all slept under the billiard table, we didn't undress and came home in the morning.

And a few days later:

I am very thankful to say we are all safe, although we have had bombs dropped too near to be comfortable. I doubt if you would recognise Garratt Lane [where we were married] and a bomb fell direct on Swaffield Road Workhouse. Penwith Road and parts of Earlsfield Road have been evacuated as there are quite a number of time bombs to go off. Most nights we don't take our clothes off at all. I would like to come down to see you but I daren't leave Mum.

From my father on 24 September:

I am sorry to tell you your car has been severely damaged by incendiary bombs although it was in Jager's garage. I cannot get any satisfaction from the company as they have been bombed out.

To add to these trials and tribulations was the shortage of food. Most things were severely rationed. Offal was 'off the ration' and huge queues would gather outside any shop that had any for sale. I can remember seeing heads of horses being delivered; they looked as if they were still alive, their eyes being open and looking quite bright. Whale meat was also in great demand.

But it is interesting to note that recent research shows that during the war the restricted diet ensured a much healthier mode of living than the unrestricted access to food, much of it having no nutritional value, that is available today.

This sort of life was not temporary, it went on for years. I wonder how many young people today realise the privations suffered and what sheer guts and determination were shown. The East End of London suffered most. Their homes were next door to some of the most important targets in England, places the Luftwaffe had to destroy if it was to bring London to a standstill. There were the dock areas, armament works, iron works, and miles of warehouses packed with food and material. The houses in this area were very old, and when the bombs fell they caught fire like matchwood.

London County Council had stored thousand of papier mâché coffins in warehouses, great pits were dug and supplies of lime assembled nearby, ready for the mass burials that were expected. However, Eastenders were more concerned with survival than being properly buried, and they had not been provided with adequate shelters. Some took refuge in a local school – where a direct hit killed 450. Some settled into an abandoned railway tunnel that ran out of Stratford Underground Station. Soon it was a cesspit, according to Superintendent Smith (Police). He was taken there by one of his sergeants. 'The first thing I heard,' Smith reported, 'was a great hollow hubbub, coughing and moaning and crying. And then a terrible stench hit me, so fetid that I gagged and then vomited. Ahead of me I could see faces lit by candles and lanterns. It was like a painting out of hell. A lot of the old folk are dying and others are dead. They do everything in there. No sanitation and no shame.' I thought this report might be an exaggeration until I read another account by an Army Lieutenant. His platoon was stationed in the South Metropolitan Gas Works, just below the Blackwall Tunnel and opposite East India Dock. On 10 July 1940 400 bombers and 600 fighters attacked the capital by day, and a further 200 bombers that night. This officer heard a bomb drop, which did not explode, probably a time bomb. He located the bomb amongst the gravestones of a churchyard. He remembered that the crypt underneath was in use as an air-raid shelter. He had to warn the occupants. It was moonlight.

> I ran down the winding steps and struggled with the door. As it burst open I was hit by a stifling wave of air so foul I retched. The temperature was like a hot house and the stench indescribable. In the dim light I saw that the stone floor was swimming in urine and between the packed human forms were piles of excrement and vomit. 112 people had been in that airless crypt for over 7 hours. I was sick myself, helplessly and endlessly.

These people had no choice, many had had their homes destroyed, it was the only way to stay alive. There was also a spontaneous evacuation: whole families dragging their belongings on wheelbarrows and bicycles, setting out to find somewhere to hide.

But things were vastly different at the other end of the social scale. Many of London's West End hotels had turned their cellars into snug shelters for patrons who had come to dine and dance and were forced to stay the night when the sirens sounded. The Duke and Duchess of Kent, Lady Diana Cooper, and other fashion leaders had bunks reserved for them at the Savoy Hotel in the event of an air raid. And not for them any austerity such as food rationing. The black market in food was flourishing; almost anything could be provided, at a price that only the very rich could afford to pay.

Little wonder then that the East End was a focus for rebellion and near mutiny. A militant procession approached the Savoy Hotel and swarmed into the posh lobby. The restaurant was closed and barricaded. Some tied themselves to pillars and others ran down to the shelters. The police were called but could do nothing.

In Liverpool, where the civil defence had completely broken down, whole areas rioted, stormed and looted food stores and wrecked Government offices. The news of all this did not leak out and even today very few people know how near England came to complete anarchy, which would have meant defeat.

In this day and age things are very different. Three years ago at Hillsborough, the home of Sheffield Wednesday's football team, a stand collapsed and many people were killed. The police dealt with the clearing up. Recently four policemen sued for damages, saying the stress and trauma they had suffered precluded them from ever working again. They were awarded very substantial damages, one of them receiving £100,000, although these awards have recently been overturned by the Court of Appeal. During the war, police, nurses, ARP wardens were pulling dead bodies out of demolished buildings day after day, month after month. When the war finished they received nothing, nor did they ever expect it. They took their uniforms off and found themselves a civilian job.

The only factor that improved morale was the performance of the RAF. Our fighters had begun to get the upper hand in the sky. Bomber Command was bombing Germany almost nightly, which gave great consolation to the victims of the Luftwaffe. Sometimes bombers took off while it was still daylight and the main force of Bomber Command was routed over London. The sight of the bombers and the roar of their engines was a terrific morale booster to the crowds below.

Chapter Seven

AT THE BEGINNING of October, I reported to 102 Squadron B Flight, which was commanded by Squadron Leader Beare. I met up with several of the lads that I had trained with, but as yet we did not know the odds that were stacked against us. We did not realise that now it was just a question of survival. We were required to complete a tour of operations, that is thirty bombing raids. Then we would be 'rested' for about six months, as flying instructors, before returning for a second tour. Then we would be grounded unless we volunteered for further raids. Strangely, of the very few who did complete sixty raids, several did volunteer and many of them eventually paid the price. The average loss on a raid was 5-10 per cent, although it was often more. If it were known by any body of fighting men that 90 or 95 per cent would return safely there is little doubt they would go into battle filled with optimism. If, however, they were told that those who returned would take part in a second battle, and then a third and so on to a total of thirty, each time losing 5-10 per cent, their optimism would have completely evaporated. The slim chance of survival would be obvious to us only after our first few raids.

Officers, 102 Squadron, 1940. F/O Cheshire middle row, 2nd from left; S/Ldr Beare front row, 4th from left.

102 Squadron was equipped with Whitley Mark V bombers. They were two-engined, very tough and could take the roughest of landings. But they were slow and did not have a high ceiling, which made them vulnerable. Down the length of the fuselage there was barely five feet of headroom and there were various obstructions, the flare-chute, Elsan toilet and wing spars.

Squadron Leader Beare gave us our first assignment. Six of us were detailed to be the funeral party at two separate funerals. A couple of nights previously the squadron had taken part in a bombing raid, and one of the planes that was landing on its return was shot down by a German intruder fighter, and as a consequence five of the crew were killed. One fellow we buried locally and it was very sad to see the terrible anguish of his wife and parents at the service. The other one we took down to a train to be transferred to his home town for burial. The policy of sending intruder aircraft to harass bombers returning to their bases was now being employed successfully. The crews, having flown for up to ten hours in a state of nervous tension, were very tired and much less vigilant. They were easy prey for the fresh German fighter pilot, who had flown from his base in Northern France in about thirty minutes.

We went into one of the hangers and saw an aircraft that had also returned from the raid. The entire side had been blown out. There had obviously been a fire on board and this aircraft had been brought back miraculously by Flying Officer Cheshire. For this episode he was later awarded the DSO. The wireless operator had been badly burned putting out the fire and he was awarded the DFM. I know

63

DY-N, piloted by F/O, returned badly damaged by anti-aircraft fire.

he was in hospital for a long time. Up till now our flying had been carefree, quite fun, but we were now beginning to realise what we had let ourselves in for. Human nature is however very optimistic. We always think it is going to happen to someone else, but never to us.

I became very friendly with a pilot named Alec Elliot and very often in the evening we went into York drinking, and during the daytime we spent many hours playing crib, because as yet we had not been allocated to any crew and most of our time was free.

102 Squadron had been bombed out from Driffield and was temporarily housed at Linton, but within a couple of weeks the whole squadron was transferred to Topcliffe, which was a comparatively new airfield that had been constructed.

I was finally crewed up with Sergeant Rix. He was a peacetime pilot, who had completed twenty-seven trips over Germany. He was very competent, very experienced and probably the best pilot that I ever flew with. He had three more operations to do to complete his first tour of thirty, and these last three would be my first three. Sergeant Stevens was the second pilot and he was also on his first operation. It was the practice for a novice pilot to fly with an experienced one for the first three or four trips in order to gain experience. Our observer, or navigator, was a Flying Officer and he also was on his first trip. But the pilot was always the actual captain of the aircraft, irrespective of his rank. Aircrews developed enormous personal loyalty to each other and had a remarkable faith in their collective ability to face the terrifying tasks that lay ahead. It is no exaggeration to say that personal safety was never considered. It was always the collective safety of the entire crew that was of prime importance.

On 21 November 1940 our crew was detailed to fly to Duisburg that night and bomb various factories there. In the morning we did our air test on O for Orange, to ensure that all the equipment was in perfect working order. At 2 o'clock we attended briefing in the main crew room and this was a very new experience for me. We were given routes to fly, wireless frequencies, met. forecasts, which incidentally were so often wrong, and areas to avoid, where intelligence knew there were fighter squadrons based or anti-aircraft locations. In fact we were given all the available information to help us on our journey there and back. In spite of what I had seen and heard, I had no feeling of fear or trepidation. That would probably arrive when I was over enemy territory and saw anti-aircraft or fighters for the first time. I didn't know what to expect, and I was a little apprehensive concerning my ability to cope with the various situations that might arise.

Take-off time was scheduled for the unearthly hour of 2.45 am, so we had a long time to hang around waiting, which was always considered to be about the worst part of the job. One bright spot was our pre-operational meal, egg and bacon, now unknown to the majority of the population. Then I went into the mess, had one or two beers and afterwards went to the library. Here I sat down quietly on my own and composed a letter to Maisie, which would only be opened in the event of me going missing. Nearly everyone did this and the letter was duly left in your flying clothing locker. In the event of you going missing, this locker would be emptied and the letter would be seen and sent off to the person to whom it had been addressed. Then the procedure was that a friend would examine all the possessions and correspondence belonging to a missing airman. Any compromising material would be destroyed. Obviously there were many illicit associations during wartime and any evidence of this received back home would cause great distress.

It should be realised that the urgency and excitement of wartime soon eroded moral restraints, and life on many home fronts appeared as cheap and short as life on the battle front. Women had also achieved some sort of liberation. No longer were they tied to the home. They were working in factories or in the services, and their men were anything from fifty to five thousand miles away, and many would be gone for years.

Many pubs and hotels employed small dance bands, and it was not unusual to see parties of women, often from the same factory, out to enjoy the music and the dancing. Of course many servicemen would be there as well. And what better time to ask a girl for a date than when you are dancing with her? 'We were not really immoral, there was a war on,' would have been the explanation for a later adulterous meeting. So persuasive was this attitude that it seemed that sexual restraint had been suspended for the duration. Many personal relationships were formed between men and women out of sheer loneliness, and the need to be loved. Most relationships of this kind were very temporary, and after the war the vast majority returned home to be loving partners and caring parents.

Though I had only been married to Maisie for less than a year, there was obviously so much you had to say when you knew that, quite likely, you were never going to meet again. A copy of this letter, recently discovered in an old kitbag follows:

29/11/40

My sweet darling Maisie,

You will see that I have put no address, so should you ever receive this letter I shall be by then beyond the reach of any written correspondence. But I thought it would be nice to leave a last letter for you, especially as things lately in the air are becoming more sticky. It is written, I am afraid, in rather a hurry, as I am visiting the Ruhr tonight and unfortunately I have not a great deal of time.

Well, my precious, I'm sorry to say that my sudden exit will cause you the sadness and heartbreaking, because I shall feel no pain & I regret to cause you suffering. But remember, my darling, a partnership like ours, which has been so full of love, so pure & unblemished cannot possibly be ended because we leave this earthly world. I am sure that I am leaving this earth which is so obsessed with sin & hate & greed to enter a much finer place, & as certain as the sun will rise tomorrow, you will join me later on. That is why I do not wish you to grieve for me, but to wait patiently for our re-union & to have absolute faith in that re-union.

Some people will consider me unlucky to die so young, but I have had twenty four years of happy life, & many people who die quite old cannot claim as much. The last two years have been the happiest of all for which, Maisie, I thank you deeply. Even though we have often been apart I have been comforted by the knowledge of our love.

68

I know you will always keep me locked not locked deeply in your heart by should you wish later to marry again, do not let my memory stop you. I do not expect my death to stop you living for all the happiness & companionship you can get.

Do all the good you can, my soul-mate, & above all have faith in God. Please do not go into mourning for me, but occasionally buy some flowers in my memory. You can be sure my last thoughts were of you, my sweet darling, who has brought me so much happiness.

Well, bye-bye, my only love, wishing you happiness until we meet again, written as always with all my love.
Doug.

This letter may seem very melodramatic today, but the circumstances merited it. I was separated from Maisie, with whom I was very much in love, and from what I had observed I was going to have to be very lucky to complete a tour of operations. Today, under the same circumstances, I would write a different letter. Gone would be my references to God, as I have lost confidence in the existence of a Supreme Being. There would be no talk of a reunion, as I now have doubts about life after death. If there is, then for me it will be an unexpected bonus. And my love for Maisie would figure even more deeply after years of companionable happiness.

In fact shortly after this time a good friend, Sergeant Mitchie, went missing and I sent his letter with a photo of him to the person to whom it was addressed, with a covering letter. I cannot recall whether it was his wife or his girlfriend. I received the following reply from her (letter in her own handwriting).

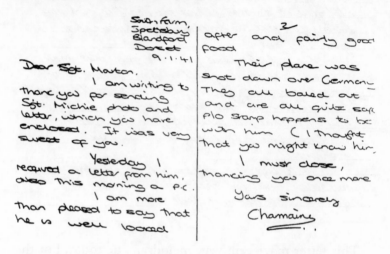

South Farm,
Spetisbury,
Blandford
Dorset
9.1.41

Dear Sgt. Marten,

I am writing to thank you for sending Sgt. Michie photo and letter, which you have enclosed. It was very sweet of you.

Yesterday I received a letter from him, also this morning a P.C. I am more than pleased to say that he is well looked

2
after and fairly good food

Their plane was shot down over Germany. They all baled out and are all quite safe. P/O Stamp happens to be with him (I thought that you might know him)

I must close, thanking you once more

Yours sincerely
Chamaine

He fortunately baled out, but he faced nearly five years as a prisoner of war. Treatment was good initially, but deteriorated later on, especially when the Germans faced defeat. I wonder what state he was in when repatriated in 1945.

Chapter Eight

WE SET OFF TO Duisburg as scheduled for my first
operation, and I was in the rear turret; a rear gunner
was the equivalent of having eyes in your behind. But it
was a very lonely position. A long way from the rest of the
crew, it was necessary to wriggle, feet first, through the
doors into the four-gun turret, then plug into the intercom
and settle down to fly backwards for however long it took.
The parachute harness was worn, but there was no room
for the parachute itself which was stowed outside the
turret. In an emergency you hoped there would be
sufficient time to evacuate the turret, locate the parachute,
attach it to the spring clips, reach the escape hatch, and
then jump. Being so far away from the rest of the crew
there was the feeling that if something very serious
occurred you might not be aware of it. But actually the
rear gunner was the most likely one to survive when an
aircraft crashed.

When we took off it was a beautiful moonlit night; the
weather was good. We had no difficulty in locating
Duisburg, duly dropped our bombs and then turned
round to come home.

Although Duisburg was in the Ruhr, which was renowned for its inhospitality, we saw very little anti-aircraft and everything had gone very well until we were returning home over the North Sea. It was then that trouble developed in one of the engines, about which I knew little, and we began to gradually lose height. When one engine fails there is always the gnawing fear of coming down in the sea. In mid-winter the North Sea is very cold and probably very rough. The dinghy has to be launched and kept stable while everyone gets in. The wireless operator would have sent out an SOS so the ditching could be located. But even then the odds against being rescued by the Air Sea Rescue Service were stacked heavily against you. Hypothermia set in after a few hours.

I could hear the anxiety in the conversation between pilot and navigator; the consolation was that Ricky was probably the best pilot on the squadron. It was decided by Ricky to make for the nearest available airfield, which was at Bircham Newton. As we had little height to spare, the airfield controller, having been alerted about our predicament, had cleared the airfield. We landed safely here, having been in the air for six hours. Mechanics attended to the engine and later that day we returned to Topcliffe. Our squadron had sent five aircraft, of which one went missing, piloted by the Squadron Commander, W/C D.R. Groom.

About this time the Italian government announced that it had taken part in the bombing of London. This caused great indignation amongst the general population and was contributory to lowering the morale of the country. A decision was therefore made by the powers that be, quite illogically, to retaliate by bombing a target in Italy, the Fiat works at Turin. Large reserve tanks were fitted into the aircraft and this lowered the bomb carrying capacity. The Whitley was not a suitable aircraft to carry out such an operation.

Previous operations to Italy had shown that they were always fraught with danger. Although the Italian defences were scorned by those more accustomed to flying to the Ruhr Valley or Berlin, the sheer distance to the target, negotiating the Alps, and the uncertainty of the weather caused Bomber Command many casualties. Seven aircraft were detailed from our squadron, and once again I was crewed up with Sergeant Rix. We set off at quarter to two in the afternoon and landed on the south coast at an airfield at Horsham St Faith, a fighter 'drome It had concrete runways, the first we had ever seen. Here we filled up again with fuel and had a meal of some sort, and set off for Italy at twenty minutes past five. We flew across France and then across Switzerland, where it was quite remarkable to see all the lights still on amongst the snow covered mountains. Isolated in the rear turret I found I was able to divide my powers of concentration into two halves. One half was devoted exclusively to keeping a sharp look out for any sign of danger, the other was free to range, appreciating the scenery or thinking about events back at the airfield or back home, wondering when I would see Maisie again. Then there were the occasional jocular exchanges over the intercom and above all the sense of 'belonging' that they brought with them, the sense of adventuring, in matchless company into space.

We did not fly over the Alps, we flew through them. At

15,000 ft. I became acutely aware of the numbing December cold that was spilling through the draughty unheated rear turret. We located the Fiat works without any difficulty and dropped our bombs. It was really poorly defended, probably by about two men and a dog.

On the way back, the met. forecast was completely wrong and instead of the skies being clear the weather was very bad, the night very black and we had great difficulty with the navigation. We were flying in 10/10ths cloud and it was impossible to get an accurate pinpoint of our position. In those days navigation was primitive; we had no radar and wireless communication was very erratic. When it was estimated that we were over England we tried to break cloud by coming down to 500 feet two or three times, quite a dangerous pursuit when you are unaware of your position, but we were not successful and now we were hopelessly lost. It is an absolute nightmare for any aircrew to be lost. It is the sheer frustration of not being able to do something to rectify the position. And there is the worry about the possibility of flying into a hill or eventually landing in the sea, so we flew round just trying to see something through some break in the cloud that would identify our position. I could hear the pilot and navigator having urgent discussions and I realised the situation was very serious.

Suddenly we were hit by anti-aircraft and we thought we were over the French coast. We turned north and were hit very badly again. We found out afterwards that we had flown over Portsmouth in the middle of a German raid and we had received priority treatment. And then we ran out of petrol. As there was no lay-by handy, the captain gave the order to abandon aircraft. In one way it was a relief. I had been cooped up for twelve hours in the rear turret, at a temperature of around −30 degrees.

My procedure should have been to leave my rear turret, put on my parachute and open the escape hatch in the roof, part way down the fuselage, climb up through it, walk along the top of the aircraft and jump off the end. However, the escape hatch would not open. It was natural that I began to feel nervous. The engines having stopped there was an eerie silence, broken only by the wind as we glided downwards. I wondered what height we still had. So with my parachute I decided to go up to the front cockpit. It was very hard to squeeze through the overload tanks that had been fitted, but I eventually got into the pilot's cockpit and there was Sergeant Rix, still at the controls. This gave my spirit a big lift. He was holding the plane steady because he was unable to find his parachute. He asked me to find it, which eventually I did. He told me to jump and I left the aircraft as quickly as possible.

It is a peculiar sensation as you jump and free fall for a few seconds; you wonder whether you have strapped your 'chute on correctly. Then you pull the rip cord, a canopy flies up past you and suddenly your speed is arrested and you are dangling in complete silence, but there is no sense of fear, and you float gently down to the ground. I was wondering where I would be landing, whether it would be in France or the Channel or England. If it was in the Channel on a cold November night there would be little hope of rescue.

Of the seven aircraft that took part in this raid from our squadron, three never even cleared the Alps and took their bombs back home. Another one forced-landed in a field near Brighton with a third ditched in the sea south off Plymouth. It was piloted by F/O Young; the crew were able to launch the dinghy and they were picked up several hours later. From then on the captain was known as 'Dinghy' Young. Unfortunately, he lost his life later, on the Dambuster raid. We had baled out, and the remaining one of the four that actually bombed Turin landed safely. It was a costly operation to lose two aircraft out of seven.

When I landed, not knowing where I was, I bundled my 'chute up and hid it in a hedge, because if I was in France I would endeavour to return to England, probably by contacting the Resistance Movement. A parachute in an open field would have been discovered by the Germans. It was 4 o'clock on a bitter November morning and I walked along until, at last, I came to a house. I knocked on the door; there was no answer, so I threw some stones up at the window, wondering where I was and even what country I was in. Soon afterwards a head popped out and said, 'Are you English, RAF or German?'

I said, 'RAF.'

'All right,' he said, 'I'll come down and let you in.'

So he came down and let me in, and I sat in one armchair, with my legs on another one, in front of the dying embers of a fire and of course I was soon asleep. I had been very relieved to know I was in England.

He woke me about 10 o'clock and asked me if he could cook me any breakfast. I was very hungry and he proceeded to cook me egg and bacon. He offered to give me a lift to the police station so that I could report. On the way we saw some men beating the woods. He stopped the car and called out to them and they said that an aircraft had crashed nearby. Four survivors had reported to the local police station at 5 o'clock in the morning, and there was still one missing. He said, 'I've got him here,' and of course that concluded their search.

Also on the way we passed our crashed aircraft. After we had taken off the previous afternoon I realised I had several letters, a photo of Maisie and other things in my pocket. This was strictly forbidden, as if one became a POW, the Gestapo could possibly glean some information from them, so I had placed them in the fuselage, thinking that if the aircraft crashed they would be destroyed. I asked the driver to stop at the crash site and when I walked to the aircraft I found everything there, exactly as I had left it Naturally, I put them back in my pocket.

Eventually we arrived at a small police station, I think it was in Midhurst, round about midday. The policeman's wife asked me if I would like any dinner. She said they usually cooked extra because there were always people dropping in on them. It was near fighter airfields and the German bomber offensive was at its peak with hundreds of aircraft being destroyed. So I had another enjoyable meal with a couple who were very helpful and sympathetic.

I obtained a railway warrant from the police station to enable me to travel back to the squadron in Yorkshire. I had to hitch-hike to the nearest main railway station and by a very strange coincidence I was given a lift by a director of the Irvin Parachute Company, who was very interested in my baling out. By baling out one becomes a member of the Caterpillar Club. The condition of membership is that you have saved your life by using a parachute, and that furthermore you had no intention of using it when you entered the plane. I received a gold caterpillar as a brooch, with SGT D R MOURTON inscribed on the back. Parachutes were made from silk, by silkworms which are actually caterpillars.

I eventually caught a train to London. It was on this journey that I experienced a peculiar feeling for the first time. A tremor seemed to pass up my back and into my head, causing me very temporarily to lose a grip of myself, almost to lose consciousness. It was probably caused by lack of sleep and the tension that I had been under. The same thing was to happen more frequently later on. I arrived in London about 9 o'clock. Maisie was living with her mum at Earlsfield so I decided that I would break my journey there. I took the underground as far as Tooting Broadway, and then walked from Tooting Broadway to Isis Street in Earlsfield, where Maisie was staying.

The front door was open and I walked through in full flying kit. Maisie was sitting at the table actually writing a letter to me and of course she was astounded when she saw me walk in. She started to ask a lot of questions. I thought it would be a better idea to go along to the Sailor Prince and have a couple of pints before they closed, which we did. Dressed as I was, I caused quite a sensation when we walked in. I was one of the heroes they had read about; I was not allowed to pay for a drink.

That night there was a very heavy German raid on the capital, so Maisie and I and her mother had to retire to the Anderson shelter and sleep there for the night. We slept on the top bunk and her mother on the lower one. When we thought it was about time she was asleep, we really made that shelter rattle. It was always the same: we always took the opportunity when it presented itself. We were very fortunate we were built the same way, with the same inclination.

It was a great temptation to stay in London for a few days, a very pleasant two or three days spent with Maisie. Eventually I decided that I had better get back to the squadron and accordingly caught a train back to Yorkshire. I went to the squadron leader's door, knocked on it, and when I walked in he said, 'Christ, Mourton, where have you been to?'

I told him I was a bit fed up and I had spent a few days in London.

He said, 'Well, there's nothing for you to fly, you had better go back there for another fifteen days. Oh, incidentally you've been posted as missing, so you had better go and collect your kit before it's taken away.' So I had a leave pass for fifteen days and went back straight away to London.

Maisie and I went to my parents' house and stayed for a couple of weeks, spending a very pleasant time there: not much to do all day and out drinking every evening. Of course, many of the people I knew had heard that I had been posted as missing and were most surprised to see us walk in the pub and order our usual drinks.

When I returned from leave our crew was given a lift down to a maintenance unit to pick up another aircraft to replace the one from which we had baled out. It necessitated staying away the night and we were booked in at a hotel in High Wycombe. It was Saturday night and we found out a dance was taking place that evening in the hotel, so naturally after a meal we joined it. The girls outnumbered the men by two to one. We were the only ones in uniform and in addition we were the glamour boys of Bomber Command, the heroes of the media and several films, so we got a wonderful welcome from the girls and had a very memorable evening. Next day reality returned and we flew our new aircraft back to Topcliffe.

On 27 November our squadron sent two aircraft to Le Havre. One went missing although this was considered a safe target. On 15 December seven made a raid on Berlin; fortunately only one failed to return. For some reason our crew had not been detailed to fly for some weeks and this was a great consolation to Maisie who wrote:

> I felt quite relieved to hear that you haven't been flying. I thought that you would do so as soon as you got back, and each night I have offered a little prayer that you might be safe. I shall go on doing so - no doubt your turn will come all too soon.

I did not operate again until 21 December, when I was promoted to wireless operator, still with Sergeant Rix as Captain. I have no recollection of what the target was, but one engine failed after we were thirty miles over the Dutch coast, so we turned around to return. Later on in the war we would have jettisoned our bombs into the sea, but in 1940 they were quite a precious commodity and were duly brought home. We steadily lost height all the way back over the North Sea, wondering whether we would make it back to England. I was busy obtaining courses to fly to arrive back to Topcliffe. We crossed the English coast, still losing height until we were almost at roof-top level. The airfield was reached and Sergeant Rix was just able to pull the plane over the boundary hedge of our airfield.

Unfortunately, on the other side there was a Whitley parked. We went right through the middle of it, cutting it in two. Our wheels and undercarriage were ripped off and it is a dangerous procedure to scrape an aircraft along the ground when it is full of high explosive and petrol. At last we came to a halt. We could not get out of the usual exit so we had to get out of the emergency exit on top of the plane. Although we were expecting that the bombs might go off at any minute, there was no panic and everybody got out of the plane in an orderly fashion. But as soon as we were all out we ran like mad for a couple of hundred yards. Then we sank to the ground, tired and out of breath. But then we started laughing uncontrollably; most likely it was the reaction setting in. Sgt. Rix had completed 27 operations without any serious trouble until I joined him. Then the last three had all ended in near catastrophe. His last remark to me was, 'Mourton, you are a bloody jinx.'

Group Captain Cheshire describes this crash in his book *Bomber Pilot* as follows:

> Jimmy and I went outside, an aircraft was approaching from the east. The aircraft came overhead and started to circle. It was a Whitley-Rix. He came through on RT asking permission to land. One engine was dead the other was running well. He still had his bombs with him. Control told him there were hostile raiders in the vicinity and to come in quickly.

The tempo of his engine quickened as he put the exacters into fine pitch. Then as he crossed the boundary marker, dead silence, he was holding off. 'Good, he's made it,' said Cheshire, 'he will be sent on rest now, deserves it too.' Then an awful rending crash and suddenly dead silence. 'That's the end of Rix,' said Cheshire.

On the aerodrome there was confused shouting and the sweep of headlights. Somewhere in the middle was a dark shapeless mass. In the dark it was impossible to make out anyone or anything. 'Put those lights out you bloody fools, there's a German overhead,' said Cheshire, 'can't you hear him? And hurry with those extinguishers.' Then Cheshire bumped into someone. It was Rix. 'Good God man, I thought you were dead.'

'Thanks. No, I'm all right,' said Rix.

'What happened?'

'There's an obstruction just by the boundary,' said Rix.

'That's no obstruction, it's N, my N, the "N". They brought it back today after putting a new fuselage on it,' said Cheshire.

(This was the aircraft with the side blown out, which we had seen when we first arrived on the squadron).

'Well, it's N no more,' said Rix, 'I hit it. I came in low on purpose because I knew we wouldn't be able to go around again on one engine. I must have misjudged it a little.'

Then a stick of bombs exploded somewhere in the direction of the hangars. Actually Cheshire was awaiting the return from this raid of his best friend, Desmond. But in fact, Desmond went missing and never did return.

Cheshire's other friend, Lofty said, 'It's always the worthwhile people who go. The scum like you and me Chesh, we stay on forever.'

'I know Lofty, don't rub it in,' said Cheshire.

DY-N cut in two by returning aircraft DY-O.

DY-O returned on one engine at night on 21 December 1940, still with bombs on board.

DY-N cut in two by returning aircraft DY-O.

Three weeks later Lofty himself went missing, Lofty, the one person in the squadron that Cheshire thought never would go. Actually, Cheshire himself went on to complete 100 operations. He was extremely efficient, completely fearless and had a wonderful sense of humour. When he was awarded the DSO he went with several officers to celebrate at a hotel in Harrogate. There was a band playing, and the music was interrupted to announce, 'Ladies and Gentlemen, I have great pleasure to let you know that F/O Leonard Cheshire is with us tonight. He has just been awarded the DSO for an act of bravery.' Chesh stood up, apparently surprised and embarrassed, acknowledging the ovation he received. One of the officers said, 'I wonder who told them,' to which Chesh replied, 'I did, you bloody fool.'

At the age of twenty-five he was promoted to Group Captain, the youngest RAF officer to achieve such high rank. But he was compelled to be chairborne rather than airborne, and later on he gladly accepted a reduction in rank to Wing Commander in order to return to operations in command of the legendary No 617 Dambusters Squadron.

He completed 103 operations and later was observer of the atom bomb attack on Japan. Then he devoted the rest of his life to Christian care of the sick and needy. It all began with an impulsive offer to take a terminally ill man into his own home and nurse him, Arthur Dykes, an old soldier dying of cancer. After him there was a 93 year-old woman, whom he gently washed every day.

Then he started the Leonard Cheshire Foundation Homes, and eventually there were 270 in 51 countries. He became Lord Cheshire in 1991, and died in 1992 at the age of seventy-four, having suffered from bad health since 1952 when he contracted tuberculosis.

Chapter Nine

S OME TWO WEEKS before this last raid, I was approached
by George Hildred, a pilot, asking me whether I would
like to share a furnished house with him, so that we could
live with our wives. It was comparatively easy to obtain
sleeping-out passes in the RAF, and we received extra pay,
theoretically to buy rations. I thought it was an excellent
idea.

He had found a furnished house in Thirsk that was
available and the rent was £2 a week. At that time £2 a
week seemed an absolutely exorbitant rate, but we took it
anyway. I wrote to Maisie outlining the plan and received
the following reply:

*On Monday I will tell Mrs Brant
that I will be going down to you
so as to give her a chance to find
someone else before I leave, please
ask about the linen also if we have
to supply our own cutlery, I will
start now to get my things ready
so that everything wont be left
until the last moment, My Darling*

*you dont know how much I am
looking forward to being with you,
you will be the smartest man in
you squad, that is if you dont go
losing your laundry ect.*

Maisie duly arrived in Thirsk, and I took her along to the house we were renting. It could only be described as reasonably adequate, but we were elated to be living together again. Any deficiencies we would overlook in our happy frame of mind.

The four of us got on so well together. Every night, when not operating, we were down the pub at 8 o'clock in the evening, staying there until they shut, getting on very well with all the locals. The four of us became particularly friendly with an old boy named Ralph and his friend, and we joined them almost every evening in the pub. Unfortunately for Ralph, his only son, who was in the navy, was killed when the *Prince of Wales* was sunk.

One evening in the pub Maisie said to me, 'I don't know what I'm going to get you for your breakfast tomorrow morning, we've got nothing.' We went home and after we had been in about ten minutes there was a knock at the door, and there appeared Ralph's friend. He had heard what Maisie had said; he was a grocer, and he had come along to give us a pound of bacon and six eggs. This showed how much our efforts were valued by the civilian population, who treated us with the greatest admiration and respect.

So the four of us carried on having a very happy life, bags of laughs. In particular, between our bedrooms there was a very narrow partition. It was possible for both couples to hear what was going on in the other bedroom, and this caused such amusement.

We managed to procure a chicken for Christmas Day's lunch. It was just as it had been killed and it needed gutting and plucking. Mary and Maisie were total novices at this sort of thing and there were feathers all over the kitchen. They had such a job to get the inside out of this chicken, but in the end we sat down to a fairly presentable meal.

That day was our first wedding anniversary, so in the evening Maisie and I decided to go into Leeds and live it up. We went down there in the car, parked it and went into a hotel where there was plenty going on and we had a really good time until about midnight. Afterwards we staggered along to the Imperial Hotel to book a room for the night. They would not believe we were married.

Here was an airman coming along with a young girl, with no luggage between them, and hotels in those days were the keepers of the morals. So they fixed us up with two single rooms on different floors. However, that did not stop us laying the keel of our first daughter, who was born the following September. Luckily I had taken my extension lead with me.

Next morning, as we approached our car, we saw there was a policeman waiting there. We were committing all sorts of offences. In those days it was not permitted to park a car after dark in the roadway. I had a Guinness bottle label in the licence disc as it was the nearest colour to a genuine licence, and I had no insurance. As he went to take down details in his notebook, I opened my great coat, ostensibly to get a cigarette, and when he saw my air crew brevet, his attitude changed immediately.

'Oh, I'm very sorry, sir, um, y-you just carry on, and good morning to you,' and off he went. This indicates once again the respect with which we were treated and how the rules could be bent.

On another occasion we went into Leeds for the evening and finished up in a hotel where a dance was being held. It was very crowded, we were all mixed up; it was difficult to see who were together. A young man asked Maisie for a dance and she accepted. He told her he was in a munitions factory earning big money and invited her back to his flat for the night. She was able to pass the information back to me, and when the dance finished he waited for her to come from the ladies cloakroom. When he met up with her she said, 'You don't mind if my husband comes as well, do you?' and I appeared on the scene. We saw the look of disappointment on his face; but he took it well. We finished up sleeping in his bed, while he slept on the settee downstairs.

Back on the squadron, Sergeant Rix had finished his tour of thirty operations and would go on rest. I met him again about twelve months later, when he was a Squadron Leader. There is no doubt that promotion was very quick indeed for those who had the luck to survive.

I had completed three operations, all of them ending in near disaster. I realised that a terrific amount of luck had to be available to be able to finish a tour of thirty. But I do not think any of us got to a state of despair, because we were young and still full of optimism.

I was now attached to the crew of Sergeant Stevens. He

was a Londoner, a Cockney, and he was very short indeed. I do not suppose he was more than 5ft 5ins, and in fact he had to have special blocks made so that he could get his feet on the rudders. He had done three trips as a second pilot, and was now the official captain of an aircraft. We went on our first operation as a crew on the day after Boxing Day 1940, to bomb the submarine base at Lorient on the west coast of France. This was considered a good, easy target for somebody who was out on their first operation as a captain. It was an unusual feeling to be going off 'on our own' for the first time. Stevie as captain would have to make all the decisions and I was in charge of the radio. I felt we had made the grade, as I expect we all did. It was a great feeling of responsibility and we were determined to do well. There were only two crews detailed from our squadron that night, both novices. As far as we were concerned, the operation went off perfectly, but unfortunately the other aircraft went missing. During these early years of the war many aircraft would be lost bombing these submarine pens. Later it was discovered that the comparatively small bombs we were dropping were quite ineffective in damaging the thick concrete that housed the submarines.

There followed two further operations with Sergeant Stevens, Bremen on 2 January 1941, which was a particularly difficult one; owing to the intense cold four of the eight aircraft despatched returned with unserviceable engines. When we reached 10,000 ft the temperature must have been around −30 degrees, and our clothing did little to alleviate the cold in the aircraft that had no heating. We encountered intense anti-aircraft fire, but returned safely.

Of the four that actually bombed, one was missing, shot down. Then we went to Brest on 12 January, which went perfectly: no trouble at all and no enemy aircraft.

On 17 January I flew with our next Squadron Commander, W/C Cole, to practise formation flying with other aircraft. I was in the rear turret and it was a frightening experience. None of the pilots had any experience of formation flying and several times the wing tip of the next Whitley came within a foot of my turret and then moved away. Formation flying is only used for daylight operations and many were the rumours circulating. Most previous daylight raids by bombers had ended in complete disaster. However, nothing came of it.

Then it snowed, and when it snows in Yorkshire it really makes a good job of it. There were mornings when I could not open the front door to get out. I had laid up my car and I was now cycling to the airfield. If I went by the proper front entrance I had to cycle right around the airfield, so I made the habit of going to the opposite side, getting through the barbed wire and then cycling around past the dispersal points to the crew room, where aircrew assembled every morning at 9 am.

I was going through the barbed wire one morning, which was totally illegal, when I ran right into an officer. Instead of taking my name, he told me to report to the guard room and he would see me there later. I never reported to the guard room, and he never managed to identify me. However, if I had been put on a charge I would have appeared in front of the Wing Commander, the man I had been crewed up with previously. He would have dealt with me as leniently as possible. On one occasion a flight sergeant put me on a charge of being improperly dressed and not carrying my gas mask. The CO gave me a really effective dressing down, but later in the day told me he had only done it to impress the flight sergeant. There was sometimes animosity between bureaucratic ground crew NCOs who had served ten or twelve years to gain their stripes and aircrew who had gained theirs in less than a year.

Owing to the snow we were unable to operate for at least three weeks. We landed and took off purely on a grass field and when this got bogged down it was impossible to take off. When we landed at night we came in with the aid of a flare path. There were no bright lights to illuminate the landing field, just some goose-necks burning paraffin that gave a very dim light. It says a lot for the efficiency and ability of the pilots that they were able to land continually with such poor aids.

Maisie and I, George and Mary were still enjoying ourselves going to the pub every evening. Because of the snow aircrews just hung about during the daytime at the airfield. I was playing cards (crib) with Sgt. Elliot regularly; it passed the time away.

However, all good things come to an end and on 4 February we were detailed to bomb Bordeaux. After we had been going along for about two hours, one engine went out of action and we were forced to return. We were unable to make it to our own airfield at Topcliffe and landed at Dishforth. When this happened, it was a particularly worrying time for Maisie. She knew that I had taken off on a raid and come the morning she knew that I had not returned. This was made worse by the fact that

she knew, or was pretty certain now, that she was going to
have a baby. It was not until midday that George was able
to get word to her that I had landed safely at another
airfield. The fault on the engine was rectified and we
returned to Topcliffe at 4 o'clock in the afternoon.

Our next trip was to Hanover. When we were briefed, it
was made clear that for the first time we were not
attacking any military targets, but were bombing a town
indiscriminately. A great shout of excited agreement
greeted the news as most aircrews had come from towns
that had suffered heavily from German air attacks.
However, my conscience was deeply concerned. I had
never volunteered to bomb civilians, to incinerate women
and children. A significant number of people felt that by
embarking on indiscriminate bombing of cities, the Allies
sacrificed something of their own moral case. I seriously
considered refusing to fly, but actually this would have
taken more guts than facing the German defences. It
would not be regarded as a conscientious objection but
cowardice, with all the shame and degradation that would
follow. We were also brainwashed although we didn't
realise it. It was impressed upon us that we were only
doing what the enemy had been doing for months. We
were told that this was the only way to bring the war to a
speedy end and thus save the lives of countless people on
both sides. But with hindsight it is clear that indiscriminate bombing only hardened the resolve of the
civilian population. Eventually I took the easy way out and
carried on. The target was given as the main post office in
the centre of the town. I was in the tail turret because a
new wireless operator was being tried out on the set. In

actual fact he could not cope and I had to take over on the return journey to get the bearings and information to enable us to land safely.

The next trip was to Sterknade oil refinery and the same arrangement took place. I was in the tail, but this time the wireless operator managed to cope with things quite satisfactorily. These trips in the tail turret were particularly boring. The turret was cramped, so you had little freedom of movement; it was very cold indeed but you dared not leave it. On the way home crews were tired, aching and stiff. We drank our coffee and ate our flying ration. We could not leave our cockpit or turrets. If we had to urinate we carried a tin, but it was very awkward. Occasionally I dozed off for a few seconds, often to wake with a start, mistaking a speck of mud on the perspex for an enemy aircraft. Several rear gunners lost fingers through frostbite when trying to clear faults in the guns, others lost the skin off their behinds when sitting on the Elsan.

On this trip, especially over the target, the anti-aircraft and the searchlights were extremely heavy and it was a very unpleasant feeling to sit in the rear turret, seeing the anti-aircraft shells bursting, sometimes near, sometimes a little farther away, and wondering whether the next one would be curtains for you. However, after eight hours flying, some of it under great stress, we landed back at Topcliffe. I had now completed nine trips and thirty still seemed an awful long way away.

We had had a succession of Squadron Commanders. Wing Commander Groom had gone missing on 21 November, when I had done my first operation. He was succeeded by W/Cdr Cole and then in March by W/Cdr Howes. He was to cause me trouble later on.

Our next trip, on 12 March, was to the big city, Berlin, the most frightening target of them all. However when we were well on our way one engine packed up and we were forced to return. We decided to bomb Hamburg as an alternative on the way back, although Hamburg raids were always dangerous.

As we approached Hamburg it was completely quiet. There were no searchlights, no anti-aircraft, nothing. We thought what a doddle it was. We carried on to the centre of Hamburg and then dropped our bombs. As soon as the bombs hit the ground, all hell was let loose. They apparently knew we were up there. They did not want to give the position of the town away, because they did not know whether we had located Hamburg or not, but as soon as the bombs actually dropped, they had us in their sights. We were coned, in the middle of several searchlights, one of the most dangerous situations, one that we always tried to avoid. When you were coned you were completely lit up. It was brighter than day inside the aircraft; you could not see. You had to get down quickly, for if you stayed in it for long you would cease to exist.

I stood petrified in the cabin, watching Stevie weave and dive and seeing the ground getting far too near for comfort. Stevie chucked the aircraft about in all directions; eventually we managed to evade the search-lights. We had dived down to about 1,000 ft, and it took a big effort by Stevie to pull the control column back to fly straight and level. We had managed to get out of trouble and returned home. Out of eight aircraft from our squadron that took part in this raid, one went missing. Another crashed on landing and two of the crew were killed. Like most raids, aircraft were lost, but you would not take too much notice. All we wanted was to get back ourselves. You got used to it, you just carried on doing your job.

The next night, we were detailed to go to Hamburg again, this time as the official target. It was a bright moonlit night and as we were approaching Hamburg, we could see another Whitley also flying along on a parallel course with us. Suddenly it exploded. What had been an aircraft a few seconds before was now a mass of debris flying through the air. It had apparently been hit by an anti-aircraft shell, most likely in its bomb bay. At times like this you realised how lucky you had been. Just two aircraft, more or less flying along together, one is destroyed, but for the other one the even money chance proved a winner. We also encountered very heavy anti-aircraft barrages, and again Stevie's ability to take severe evasive action saved us. But at the climax of every trip came the long run-up to bomb, through the dazzling web of lights, the flicker of flak, the curling twisting pattern of the tracer and the glow of the fires below.

There had only been three aircraft taking part from our squadron and next morning I found out that the one that had gone missing was piloted by my very best friend on the squadron, Alec Elliott. He was the man who, before Maisie had come to live with me, I had gone out drinking with every night. We used to play crib day after day, waiting in the crew room, and I had seen him go. He had lent me a book, *Gone with the Wind*, which, of course, I would be unable to return to him. To lose a good friend was initially very distressing. But such was the pace of our losses, we soon forgot, and it served to emphasise how lucky we ourselves had been.

Our next trip was on to Bremen. This was comparatively easy because we did not have to fly over any German territory and of the seven aircraft that went and took part, all returned safely. During the last two trips, we had been accompanied by Wing Commander Howes as second pilot. He was the CO whom I mentioned earlier. Rumour had it that he had been chairborne at Air Ministry for some years and had not flown an aircraft during the whole of that time.

The next evening Stevie was detailed to give Wing Commander Howes tuition on take-offs and landings and I had to accompany them as wireless operator. The first landing that W/C Howes made by himself was almost catastrophic. He came down and hit the deck going much too fast; the aircraft bounced up to about 50 feet and hovered there. Stevie opened the throttle straight away and the aircraft sort of hung there deciding whether to go on or just flop onto the ground. Fortunately it went off okay and we went round again. Next time when he came in to land, he went much too far down the field and we went through the boundary fence and landed in a ploughed field.

Squadron Commanders only flew on operations now and again, so consequently they never had a permanent crew. One day I heard someone in the crew room say, 'I don't want to go for a burton [get killed] but if I do, I hope it's with W/Cdr Howes.' Wing Commander Howes was a self-confident man and he actually put himself down to fly on the next operation, which was to Berlin. By now, having done twelve operations, I was the longest surviving wireless operator/air gunner on the squadron and the one with the most experience. To my horror he put me down to fly as his wireless operator. I must admit I was really dead scared. He was a poor pilot and Berlin was probably the toughest target of all. I reported sick, but the MO just told me that if the pains in my stomach continued, to come back next week. It was the first and only time that I ever tried to evade my responsibility. Fortunately, later that evening the operation was cancelled due to bad weather.

The next day I was detailed once again to fly with Wing Commander Howes. This time the target was Lorient in France, a comparatively easy target. As far as we were concerned everything went well, but again, out of the seven aircraft that took part, there was one that had gone missing.

I knew that Wing Commander Howes would not be flying again for at least a month, which was quite a relief. Back again I was crewed up with Sergeant Stevens. This was on 23 March and the target was once again Berlin. However, once again we never made it, and again we bombed Hamburg as the alternative. Looking back now I wonder if we really did have to turn back each time Berlin was the target, or whether Stevie considered discretion was the better part of valour. Out of the three aircraft that took off that evening from our flight, only two actually located Berlin and one of these was shot down.

Chapter Ten

IT IS PROBABLY RIGHT to look at the conditions under which we were operating. The overwhelming majority of crews who operated during the autumn of 1940 and through 1941 were conscientious airmen who did their best to find and hit their targets, but we were operating under tremendous difficulties. We were not equipped with radar or any other sophisticated navigational aids.

The aircraft were fitted with inadequate ancillary equipment. The only navigational aids the navigator was supplied with were a sextant and a compass. The aircraft were without heating and the cold was appalling. The crews flew clothed in layers of silk, wool and leather and yet they were still bitterly cold. Vital systems jammed, wings iced up for lack of adequate de-icing gear, guns froze and the crew's limbs seized with the cold.

The navigator gave his pilot a course on take-off and then relied upon dead reckoning navigation, hoping to be able to establish pin-points on the ground below at intervals in the seven or eight hour flight. When visiting Germany we always flew out over Flamborough Head, then across the North Sea to the Frisian Islands, off the

Dutch coast. If visibility was satisfactory, both these places gave a good pin-point. However, as a counter-move, Germany placed a fighter squadron on the islands, enabling their aircraft to fly into the bomber stream and successfully shoot some down.

If the night was clear and the stars could be seen, then it was possible for the navigator to obtain a fix with his sextant, provided the pilot was willing to fly straight and level for long enough. That could be a dangerous operation.

It was sometimes possible for the wireless operator to obtain a loop bearing from England, but the bearing could often put the aircraft on a 180 degree reciprocal course. The Germans also jammed the wave-lengths. Navigators were given the weather forecast before take-off, which included predicted winds. Often the predictions were inaccurate and the winds were blowing the aircraft off track. The crews could attempt to check drift by dropping a flare, which was at best a chancy business and quite impossible in low cloud.

Obviously, therefore, if it was a cloudy night it was necessary to rely on dead reckoning, but there were several factors that could cause serious errors, and again and again during this period the enemy were unaware that Bomber Command had been attempting to attack a specific target. Bombs were being dropped all over Germany, in villages, farms and homes, as well as on factories and industrial regions.

Our bombing operations were not nearly as effective as the official reports and the media claimed. However, the most important point was that we were keeping up the morale of our civilian population. Our armies had been overwhelmed in France and rescued from Dunkerque, our navy was suffering severe losses, and German bombers were creating havoc and despair with their regular raids on our towns, as they only had to travel a few miles from their airfields in France. The extracts from letters received by me on pages 55 and 56 illustrate the strain that was being experienced by the civilians. The only gleam of hope the population had was to read of the exaggerated reports of the RAF bombing raids on Germany.

It was also estimated that over a million Germans were employed on searchlights, anti-aircraft gun sites, first aid stations and fire stations who would otherwise have been available for the fighting at the front.

It was on the return journey that the wireless operator became one of the most important people in the crew. He was the one who, when coming across the North Sea, could obtain a fix from one of the radio stations in England. The only trouble was there were very often fifty or a hundred aircraft, all trying to do the same thing, and it was only the wireless operators who calibrated their set very accurately who received a response from the radio stations. In very serious circumstances he could send an SOS.

At the beginning of April, I found myself crewed up with another pilot, Sergeant Doherty. He was an Irishman who had not flown on operations as a captain so far, and I presume that I was crewed up with him so as to give him the benefit of my experience. We were detailed to fly on operations on 1 and 2 April, but at the last minute both of these operations were cancelled. This was particularly stressful, as during the day we had done an air test on the aircraft, flying around for probably half an hour to an hour, making sure that all the equipment was in perfect order. We attended the briefing in the afternoon and then hung around for several hours and then just before take-off the whole thing was scrubbed.

However, on 3 April we were detailed to fly to Brest and actually took off. We had been flying for two or three hours when our intercom system failed. We were flying just above a bank of clouds when a German fighter was sighted. We immediately dived into cloud cover, because the task of a bomber was to carry out the raid, to evade fighters and only seek combat when unavoidable. Inside the cloud we ran into an electric storm. Sparks were flying off the propellers, there were bangs and crackles, a most eerie experience. Then one engine was struck by lightning and packed up. We had no alternative but to turn back and jettison our bombs. This then became a very tough assignment for Sergeant Doherty, being his first operation as captain of the aircraft. Actually, without boasting, I can say it was a good thing that he had an experienced wireless operator with him that night, because I was able consistently to get courses to steer to take us back to England.

We were losing height across the Channel and I was able to get permission to land at Tangmere, which was on the south coast, and also give him courses to steer to arrive there. We landed safely. Of the aircraft that took part in this raid, none were actually lost over the target, but one aircraft apparently also got into difficulties in the same way as we did. They crashed on landing and they were all killed. Once again, Maisie had the worry of wondering whether I was missing or whether I had landed at another airfield.

It was near midnight when we landed at Tangmere. We were not provided with any beds, but were given an egg and bacon supper and then we just lay about in the sergeants' mess waiting for the morning to come. Our aircraft was eventually repaired and we landed back the next afternoon. Apparently Sergeant Doherty was now allocated a permanent wireless operator and I went back to flying with Sergeant Stevens, which suited me very well.

On 7 April we were detailed to fly to Kiel. This was a particularly long trip across the North Sea, but it had the advantage that we did not fly over much German territory. The visibility that night was extremely good. It was bright moonlight and we observed our bombs hitting the docks, which was our target. Kiel was a particularly long haul back and I was very busy on the return journey getting courses to fly; eventually we landed safely after seven hours. Seven aircraft went out that night from our squadron and one went missing. We had arrived back at 4 o'clock in the morning. By the time we were de-briefed, had our meal and I had gone home and got into bed, it was gone 6 o'clock, but a despatch rider came around about 9 o'clock and told Maisie I was detailed to fly again that night. She woke me up and, very weary and heavy, I reported to the airfield. I had been up almost twenty-four hours the previous day, much of it under great stress, and after a couple of hours actual sleep I was due for another long stint.

Once again Kiel was the target. Apparently, the raid the

previous night had been so successful that they decided to make use once again of the bright moonlight and the northern lights. Ten aircraft from our squadron took part, but four never made it. I had now completed seventeen trips out of the thirty. I was the most experienced wireless operator on the squadron, and I was beginning to see the light at the end of the tunnel, because having completed seventeen, another thirteen seemed quite possible.

Next followed a trip on Düsseldorf, which was a piece of cake. Eight aircraft took part; they all bombed successfully and returned home, which was unusual because the Ruhr was considered particularly hazardous.

The next operation on 12 April was to Bordeaux. It is quite a long haul when circumstances are good, but this particular night we had difficulty with navigation. It took us a long while to locate Bordeaux and the navigator had problems on the way back. As a consequence, flying over France our petrol reserves were becoming dangerously low. I was kept very busy on the wireless getting homings from Abingdon and we landed there, having been in the air for ten hours and with our petrol almost exhausted. Once again, though, it was a good night in general. Six aircraft took part and all returned safely. We landed at 6 o'clock in the morning, refuelled and took off again at 8 o'clock. Once again, Maisie was overjoyed when I returned back to Topcliffe.

On 15 April we returned once again to Kiel. From our point of view the trip was uneventful, but of the seven aircraft from our squadron that took part, two got bogged down in the mud before take-off, two returned without having found the target, and of the three that actually got to Kiel, one was shot down. So out of the seven aircraft only our crew and one other had a satisfactory journey.

On 17 April Berlin was the target. It was a long, arduous and nerve-racking flight and after nine hours flying, we returned home safely to base. It must be emphasised that most of the nine hours were spent in a state of hypertension. Having crossed the Dutch coast anti-aircraft was encountered on the way to Berlin, and when you were about fifty miles from the target it seemed impossible to penetrate the barrage that surrounded it. Searchlights had to be evaded and seeing the occasional bomber being shot down in flames obviously heightened the tension. The pilot would be weaving and turning all the time, and all of us would be on a continual lookout for fighters. Of the eight aircraft from our squadron that took part that night, one sent a SOS that he was landing in the North Sea and was never heard of again, and in addition to that, one other aircraft was missing. Once again, losing two crews out of eight emphasised how the odds were stacked against completing thirty operations.

On 25 April Wing Commander Howes decided that he would operate once again and I was very disturbed to find that he had selected me as his wireless operator. The target was Kiel. It all went off uneventfully however and of the ten aircraft that took part, all returned safely.

Our Flight Commander had gone missing a couple of weeks previously and at the end of April we received a new one, Squadron Leader Burnett. He was commencing his tour of operations and I found that I was crewed up with him. Once again I had been chosen because I was the most experienced wireless operator on the squadron. So

Damaged rear turret, 2 May 1941.

on 30 April, again the target was Kiel, but this time with Squadron Leader Burnett. As far as we were concerned the operation was a complete success.

April had been an extremely good month for me. I had completed nine operations and was now well on my way to the end of my tour. On 2 May I was crewed up once again with Squadron Leader Burnett and the target was Hamburg. It turned out to be one of the most nerve-racking flights I had taken part in. That night I learnt that Squadron Leader Burnett was one of the 'press it home at all costs' type of man.

The anti-aircraft that night over Hamburg was particularly heavy and on the run up to the target we were coned in about twelve searchlights. It was so bright it was impossible to see. If Stevens had been the pilot, he would have shouted to the bomb aimer, 'Drop those bloody bombs and let's piss off home!' but Squadron Leader Burnett was made of different stuff. He turned the aircraft round into an acute dive. Still the searchlights held us and we knew that if we were held too long, we were obviously going to be shot down by a fighter or by anti-aircraft. However, he continued to weave and dive until eventually we lost the searchlights, but we were now almost on top of the houses in Hamburg. It took the two pilots all their strength on the control column to pull it out of the dive.

To my dismay, he said to the navigator, 'I'm climbing to 12,000 feet and I want you to give me a course to steer to go in again.' Laboriously, with a full bomb load on, we climbed to 12,000 feet and the navigator gave him the course. We were on a straight and level course to bomb the docks but the majority of aircraft had now left and once again the searchlights came on us and the anti-aircraft began noisily banging all around us. Somehow we got out of it, but it was purely by luck, and eventually we left the target area and returned home. Of the ten aircraft that took part that night, one was missing.

Digressing a little, quite by chance I received another account of this actual flight. I recently read a letter from Philip Brett in *Intercom*, an air crew magazine. I recognised the name, wrote to him and confirmed he was on 102 Squadron at the same time as I was. After several letters, we spent the weekend at his house, reminiscing on events that happened over fifty years ago.

Then I was surprised to receive another letter from him:

But now Sir Douglas – to come to the real reason for this longer epistle. You were quite right in stressing the amazing – almost unbelievable – coincidence with our survival careers in the RAF, but I'm sure you hadn't realised (and I had missed) the final even more amazing chapter in this saga. Oh yes! we both knew your friend ?? W/C Howes, and OH yes! we had both flown with S/Ldr Burnett, but – and here comes a very big but – *we both flew together with S/Ldr Burnett on the same two operations.* My very first Op (Kiel) on the 30th April 1941 as Rear Gunner with him, also had a certain Sgt. D. Mourton as W/Op and the next one on the 2nd May, to Hamburg again as Rear Gunner, also had a Sgt. Mourton as W/Op. I had no idea of this until I was looking through a diary I had written, and realised that here was the final amazing little piece of the jigsaw.

You mention in your 'book' that this Hamburg one was one of the most nerve-racking of the lot, and I can confirm that it certainly shook me up in the rear turret, especially on only my second trip. Even in the diary I wrote about it, I commented . . .

'we approached the target at about 17,000 feet and caught in a few s/l [searchlights] and thereafter we were immediately coned. Our skipper tried everything to get away, but no luck and we were being plastered with heavy flak. Then suddenly the a/c was hurled in a screaming dive. The vibration in the rear turret was unbelievable, and I completely lost all sense of direction, and at one time even imagined we were upside down, as some s/l seemed to be shining from above, but after ages we were free of their attention, and we went in again . . .' I even said that '. . . on our quiet trip back over the North Sea our W/Op climbed along the fuselage to see the extent of the damage, with the a/c riddled with flak holes, but thankfully missing all the vital parts, and we settled down for a quiet trip the rest of the way home . . . ' The W/Op must, of course, have been you . . . how about that!!!

So it just goes to show what a really incredible final chapter we had, it must be great odds against finding such a sequence and such a reunion after all this time.

I was also pleased to read that you had written to a daily paper about the controversy over BC's [Bomber Command] effort in the war, but disgusted that they didn't print your letters. That's what makes me so mad – we should be so proud of the whole thing (as I am) but everyone else wants to pretend it never happened . . . I shall still write again, sometime, when I get mad again. Whitleys and 1941 will get just recognition one day. All strength to your elbow Sir D . . . '

Receiving this letter was indeed a great surprise to me. Of all the people that I met during the six years of war, Philip is the only one that I have been able to contact.

It was about this time that I began having trouble with my ears. They were discharging blood on the pillow when I slept. I think that when sometimes we dropped 10,000 feet in about ten seconds, the difference in pressure was causing a problem. I was also having nightmares and Maisie sometimes had to wake me up, because I was moaning and shouting.

Two days afterwards, I was crewed up once again with Squadron Leader Burnett. The target was Brest, a very easy one, but it was nice to get there and back without incident. Six aircraft took part and all returned safely.

On 9 May, my birthday, I found myself crewed up yet again with a fresh pilot, a Sergeant Dougall. It was obvious that I was being crewed up with pilots who were just beginning their tour of operations which was a little disconcerting as the majority of losses were from pilots who were on their first five trips. So if you flew with a pilot on his very first operation, the odds were stacked against you more than usual. Our target was Mannheim but it was an easy trip and I was kept busy on the return getting courses to fly. One aircraft failed to return. On 11 May, again with Sergeant Dougall, we went to Bremen and got home without incident.

I had now completed twenty-seven trips, but was getting to the jittery stage, which happened when you had only two or three more trips to complete. However, two days afterwards, to my surprise, the Flight Commander came into the crew room and informed me that I had completed my tour. Apparently, a new Air Ministry directive had just been issued saying that when 200 operational hours had been completed, the tour was finished, irrespective of the number of operations flown. This was to recompense those people who had flown a high percentage of long arduous trips. He wished me the best of luck and said that he was recommending me for the award of the Distinguished Flying Medal. In a lot of cases this medal was not given for any specific act of bravery, but just as a reward for a tour of operations. It became known as the Survivors' Medal.

Chapter Eleven

THE FEELING OF RELIEF at the completion of a tour of operations is indescribable, especially as we were expecting our baby. You realised your chance of survival had increased. The usual procedure was to be posted as an instructor to an OTU (Operational Training Unit). You knew that in the normal course of events you would be required to complete a further tour of operations after probably nine months or so of instructing. However that bridge would be crossed in due time, no point in worrying about it. Naturally we celebrated the completion in the company of George and Mary and all our friends at the local pub.

The end of a tour is probably the time for some reflection. Almost all my friends had gone missing. The remarkable thing is that you felt no sense of loss, you did not grieve, and in a week or two you had forgotten they ever existed. I think it was because it happened so regularly and you eased your conscience by thinking they were probably prisoners of war. Of course one had the 'I'm all right, Jack' mentality. Also, in Bomber Command you rarely saw a dead body – names were rubbed off the board in the Operations Room and people failed to turn up at breakfast next morning. It was at debriefing after a raid that you realised who had 'gone for a burton' (gone missing). All aircraft that had gone on the raid were listed on a board, under the captain's name. You could tell by the blanks who had not come back, although some might have made emergency landings or baled out. After going to bed and returning you got the full true story. It was inevitable that we became hardened to loss.

Looking back I am amazed at the flippant way we went about our dangerous business. In the crew room before an operation, the atmosphere was such that you would have thought we were about to take a holiday trip to Spain, plenty of banter and leg-pulling, completely unforced laughter. Probably three crews would jump into a transport to be taken to the aircraft, plenty of chat with the WAAF driver. The only serious ones seemed to be the ground crews, worried that their protégés (the crew and the aircraft) might not return.

Regarding the trouble I had with Wing Commander Howes, I will relate an incident that happened at the beginning of April, soon after I was crewed up with Sergeant Doherty. The wireless receiver 10-82 and transmitter 10-83, which we had been using since the beginning of the war, were replaced with the 11-54 and 11-55. These were considered much superior. On 1 April, I did a comprehensive air test for an hour and a half and I gave the new sets a really good try-out and found they were very satisfactory.

We were informed that there were operations scheduled for that night and in the afternoon we went along for the briefing. The target was Berlin and our Squadron had been ordered to make an all-out effort and put up as many aircraft as possible. That evening we got into the aircraft as usual and on our way taxiing around the airfield I tried out the radio which was quite normal procedure. It was completely dead. I could not get anything on it at all. It was remarkable, as it had behaved so well during the morning. But I informed the pilot, Sergeant Doherty, and he said he had no alternative but to scrub the operation.

We returned to the operations room and I was immediately confronted by Wing Commander Howes, whom I have referred to previously. He was in a hell of a temper, quite livid and beside himself. He accused me of lack of moral fibre, which was the RAF term for cowardice, and then went on to say that he would have me shot for cowardice in the face of the enemy. I had already completed fourteen operations and was anxious to complete my tour. He was in such a state that I knew I dared not utter a word, because I was sure he would have had me put in the guard room and later court-martialled. I knew it would have been very difficult to prove my innocence. My only consolation was that I could see the look of sympathy on the faces of all the WAAF and RAF who were also in the operations room.

The reason he was so mad was that he wanted the honour and glory of putting a record number of aircraft from our squadron into the air. The outcome was that next morning the signals officer approached me and apologised. He said that the new sets had been put in wrongly on my aircraft and that while they were on the ground they were earthed, but while they were in the air they were quite satisfactory. I told him that he had better tell the Wing Commander, but of course he never did, because the correct operation of the radios was his responsibility. That was why I was never actually awarded the DFM, because the Wing Commander would have had to countersign the Flight Commander's approval.

After I completed my tour of operations at Topcliffe, I was informed that I had been posted to Driffield. However, I was very happy at Topcliffe with Maisie and I hesitated to leave. I had contacted someone I knew in Driffield and every couple of days I would phone up to find out whether there had been any panic about my non arrival. But after about ten days I moved on.

Having completed my tour of operations. I was promoted to Flight Sergeant with a massive shilling a day increase in pay. My job at Driffield was to instruct 104 Squadron wireless operators who had just arrived on the squadron and had no real knowledge of operational flying. Within two days of arriving on 104 Squadron however I was crewed up with a Pilot Officer Jones. They were short of a wireless operator/air gunner. The target was Cologne.

This was the first time I had flown in a Wellington and I was the front gunner, a very nerve-racking experience. After climbing into the front turret, you realised that you were unable to get out, unless another member of the crew opened the door for you. You also left your parachute behind in the cabin. Having baled out once, this was a very unpleasant feeling. I could imagine, in an emergency, the crew baling out in a hurry and leaving me behind. You felt utterly and completely unprotected and you could not see what use you were in the front turret anyway, as attacks always occurred at the rear of the aircraft. Right at the nose of the aircraft, feeling almost naked, with a first class view of the anti-aircraft barrage we were about to enter, it was a very nasty experience. However the trip went off without incident, and it would be the last operation for me for some months.

I was now allocated a classroom, a blackboard and a desk and left to my own devices to give the benefit of my experience to the new wireless operators. Sometimes I regaled my pupils with details of my exploits, often a little exaggerated, and my caterpillar badge worn on my lapel added to my reputation. I was regarded almost with reverence. There was no official to check on me; I could come and go almost as I pleased – a real cushy number.

My problem now was finding accommodation and also getting another sleeping-out pass. Eventually I contacted Mrs Tate, who lived in a council house in Driffield and whose husband was in the Eighth Army fighting in North Africa. We took the front room downstairs and the front room upstairs for our bedroom. The accommodation was very pleasant, and Mrs Tate was very easy to get along with. Actually she had hesitated to let rooms at first, as it was apparently against Council rules. She had one child, a boy about six years old. I would often play with him and amuse him, a very likeable lad.

Maisie was now almost six months pregnant, but she did not show very much and as a consequence we had not told Mrs Tate that we were expecting a baby. We hesitated a long while before breaking the news to her, as we feared that she might ask us to go. However her words were, 'Well, you've got to have the bairn somewhere, so you might as well have it here.' So our immediate worries were at an end and we settled in very comfortably.

I even took an allotment at the end of the road and started cultivating vegetables. And of course we were down the pub every evening making friends with the locals.

In 1941 there was little in the way of ante-natal attention or information and the first time Maisie went along to St Mary's Hospital was about four weeks before the baby was due. They measured her hips, said that everything should be satisfactory and told her to come back again when the pains started. However, they said she would receive special attention as she only had one kidney.

We found living conditions at Driffield very pleasant indeed. I did not have a lot of work to do and no-one seemed to check on me. I was tending my allotment quite a lot. On my actual days off we were going down to a nearby river and taking a picnic. It was warm and I often enjoyed a swim. In spite of Maisie's condition we went on long walks in the evening through the countryside. During the war we had double summer time, so the sun set very late.

In 1941 rationing was very strict indeed. I was lunching in the sergeants mess, quite unofficially, every day and this managed to eke out our rations, especially as far as meat was concerned. We were very friendly with a farm worker whom we met in the local pub. He would very often bring us pig's chitterlings, that is the heart, the liver and the inside linings of a pig's stomach, in an old tin can. I do not suppose many people have even heard of pig's chitterlings and probably would not eat them if they were offered, but when they are fried with onions they make a very succulent dish. Maisie would often line up outside the tobacconist to buy cigarettes for me; the maximum amount being sold was five to each person, they were in such short supply.

On 11 September Maisie and I went along to the local cinema, taking with us a pound of plums. As it happened Maisie ate the majority of these. That night about 1 o'clock she awoke with pains and she thought that it was the plums that she had eaten earlier in the evening. It persisted and we woke Mrs Tate, who gave us the benefit of her experience. This was labour pains, she decided, and we would have to go along to the hospital as soon as possible. There was no way of getting a taxi, no way of getting an ambulance: we had to walk to the hospital, which was over a mile away. I well remember it was about 2 or 3 o'clock in the morning; President Roosevelt was giving an important speech and obviously most people in England were very interested. As a consequence, as we walked along the road in the middle of the night there were many houses with their lights switched on. Maisie was in great pain and we would stop every fifty yards or so and she would cling to the railings and bite her teeth, then we would carry on again and eventually we reached St Mary's Hospital about 4 o'clock in the morning.

Such were the conditions then, that one girl had had a long walk and had actually given birth to her baby in her knickers. I saw Maisie into the hospital. Next morning I got up early to pay a visit before I went down to the airfield. I arrived at the hospital about half past seven and to my delight Maisie was sitting up in bed nursing our first born, Pat. Only having one kidney had not caused any problems; it had been quite a normal delivery. I said to her, 'My word, there's nothing in it. It's a piece of cake,' but she soon corrected me about this.

Of course I visited Maisie regularly, and on one particular evening an unusual thing happened. I was sitting by the side of her bed, probably recounting the events of the day, when I jumped two feet in the air. A wasp had climbed up my leg and stung me in the testicles. It was very painful, so painful that I had to accept the nurse's offer of first aid. Quite embarrassing.

Maisie was in hospital for a week, and had a happy home-coming. Mrs Tate had cooked a lovely meal for us all, and also put a bunch of flowers on our living room table. She was a very sweet person. It was almost a party atmosphere.

I do not know whether prams were unobtainable or whether we could not afford one, but the one we had was sent up by my mother by rail and had been used by my cousin. Maisie's mother had arranged to stay with us for a while, probably, we thought, to supervise. When she arrived Maisie was outside washing down the pram, and she received a severe scolding from her mother for putting her hands in cold water so soon after having a baby. She stayed with us for a couple of weeks and was a great source of information and help. Maisie lost her milk after only a few weeks, probably because of the very stringent rationing and the lack of nourishing food. There were no baby foods available of any description, but we did get a milk ration. We fed Pat on cow's milk, which we brought to the boil and added lime water, so as to give strength to her bones and later on to her teeth, and sugar. I made enough feed for the whole day every morning before I went down to the airfield.

I had had more experience of babies than Maisie, because I was eight years old when my brother had been born and I was quite capable of changing napkins and bathing a baby. Apart from that we were both very inexperienced and we did rely, to a large extent, on the advice of Mrs Tate.

Sometimes on a Sunday we would pool all our meat rations and have a meal together. If possible we would get a small joint of beef. Mrs Tate would cook it in the traditional Yorkshire method. The beef would be roasted in the oven on bars with a Yorkshire pudding immediately underneath. The juices and fat would drop onto the pudding which provided a very succulent course to be eaten before the main meal. It was a good filler-up.

The period of inactivity as far as flying was concerned came to an end abruptly on 30 November. I was crewed up with a Sergeant Warnock for a raid on Emden. Actually, it was the thirtieth trip of his tour. He was a very efficient and experienced pilot, very cool even when things did not go quite right, and this trip was one of the best I had taken part in. Once again I was in the front turret of a Wellington but on the way back the wireless operator could not cope and I was transferred into his position. The raid went off very smoothly indeed and took only five hours. Tragically, a few months after completing his tour of operations Sergeant Warnock was killed in a flying accident while instructing (see page 131). This was to be my last operational trip at Driffield and would finish my operational flying until the following May.

I had been particularly lucky. In 1940/41 very few aircrew finished a tour of operations. Later on the chances improved to one in three. Other statistics show that we started the war with 500 bombers, 10,000 were produced and we finished with 1,500. On Bomber Command 55,000 were killed, although the number to operate on any particular night was anything between 1,000 and 7,000 only, until almost the end of the war when large numbers of bombers had been produced. I regularly attend reunions of 102 and 104 Squadrons, Air Crew Association, Bomber Command Association, but only on two occasions have I met anyone who commenced operating in 1940.

102 Squadron, with whom I completed the tour of operations, was equipped with Whitley Mark Vs. It was a two engined aircraft, sturdily built of metal, but only cruised at 160 m.p.h. and it was nicknamed 'the Flying Coffin'. The rear turret was equipped with four Browning .303 machine guns with a range of 400 yards. On a winter's night it was the coldest place on earth. 104 Squadron was equipped with Wellington 3s, also two engined, which had a rear turret with four Browning .303s. It cruised at 180 m.p.h., but it had a fabric body which was vulnerable and caught fire very easily.

German fighters were equipped with .5 cannons with a range of 800 yards. They usually attacked from behind or underneath, firing upwards, and were rarely seen before the attack took place. Bombers never attempted to take on fighters except when attacked. Our job was to see the fighters first, and a rear gunner would instruct his captain which way to turn and dive or climb to get out of trouble.

It was unbelievable the state in which some aircraft arrived home: on one engine, large parts of the wings missing, undercarriage shot away, etc. Bailing out over enemy territory was only done as a last resort. Great risks were taken by crews to bring a badly damaged aircraft home.

Chapter Twelve

ALL GOOD THINGS eventually come to an end, and just before Christmas 1941 I was posted to an Operational Training Unit, or OTU as we called it, at Wellesbourne near Stratford-on-Avon. This brought to an end a very pleasant eight months at Driffield, with a lovely person, Mrs Tate. Maisie and I were both very disappointed to be separated again, especially as our little girl was now three months old. Over fifty years on we still remember Driffield and Mrs Tate with great affection.

It was a long journey down to Stratford from Driffield and I arrived there about 8 o'clock in the evening. I was very hungry but food had finished. My posting here was as a Wireless Operator Instructor, not behind a desk as I had been at Driffield, but actually flying with my pupils. An OTU should be a safe enough place, but we were flying with dodgy crews in dodgy aircraft. The aircraft were Wellington 1Cs which were very old and obsolete, and old aircraft were always at greatest risk. All flying in those days was dangerous, and throughout the war 8,300 lost their lives on training establishments.

That evening I had a look around the sergeants mess.

There was nobody at all that I knew and I felt very down-hearted. I had left Maisie and Pat behind just before Christmas, and just before our second wedding anniversary. I then saw a notice on the notice board about a recital of Handel's *Messiah* that was being given at the local church, so I went along there and had a reasonably pleasant evening listening to it.

Next morning when I went down to breakfast I was highly delighted to meet Jock Cullen and Mac, two wireless operators with whom I had been very friendly on 102 Squadron. They confirmed what I already knew, that instructing on an Operational Training Unit was no picnic. The accident rate at Operational Training Units was appalling. Some courses lost as many as 25 per cent of their trainees, and of course many instructors went with them. It was anything but a rest-cure for men who had completed a tour of operations. In fact, a couple of weeks previously, two aircraft had crashed on landing in a snow-storm; five had been killed and four seriously injured. Although we were not on an operational squadron, we were still very much in the front line. No 22 Operational Training Unit was being used to train Canadian air crews. We looked upon them with some envy, as their pay was almost double ours and they received many parcels from home containing food and hundreds of cigarettes and other delectable items.

Almost immediately Jock, Mac and I were posted to a satellite of Wellesbourne called Atherstone, later renamed Stratford Airfield. This airfield had been thrown together in rather a hurry and living conditions were very spartan, especially during this very cold winter. Instructors were billeted in two-bed huts and Jock and I settled into one of them. I could not have asked for a better room-mate. We had both completed an operational tour as W/OP/AGs, we had the same outlook on life and we thought along the same lines. He was a wonderful pal, and it is one of my deepest regrets that I finally lost touch with him.

The heating was a solid fuel stove at the end of the hut and our allowance was one scuttleful of coal a week. This was totally inadequate, but Jock and I soon found the location of the coal-dump. It had a very high wire fence around it, angled at the top, but every evening after dark we managed to climb over and fill up our scuttle. Then we took it in turns to get up in the night to replenish the fire.

There was no hot water in the showers, and ablutions were about fifty yards away from our huts. If you wanted a shower, you stripped off in the hut, went across to the shower with a towel around you, showered in cold water and then came back again. Naturally we did not shower very often.

On 3 January another crew crashed on landing and three more were killed and two were injured. The accidents were being caused partly through poor aircraft, and partly due to the inexperience of the crews that were flying them.

Jock, Mac and I and several others often went in the evenings to local towns to a pub or a dance or any other means of entertainment. Usually the time the last bus left did not fit in with our arrangements, and sometimes we slept at the YMCA, sometimes in a railway carriage, or even on a station platform with a gas mask as our pillow. Then we would get up early and hitchhike back to camp.

The pubs in Stratford shut about half-an-hour after the last bus left for the airfield, and as a consequence many airmen were left stranded and in no condition to walk the six-mile journey back. Anything was stolen (borrowed) to get back, mostly bikes but on more than one occasion a bus. The police regularly collected the borrowed articles the next morning.

I began my usual search for accommodation, so that Maisie and Pat could join me. Eventually I located two rooms that were available in a farmhouse at the top of a very steep hill called Atherstone-on-the-Hill. So I applied for a living-out pass and also a weekend pass to go and collect Maisie and Pat.

It was a bitterly cold morning when we started off from Driffield. There had been heavy falls of snow and when we moved from one accommodation to another we had to take the whole of our worldly possessions with us. There was the pram with the baby in it, my bicycle, all our clothes, the cot, the radio: in fact we were completely fully loaded.

We started off very early in the morning. We went from Driffield to York, changed trains, and then travelled from York down to Snowhill, Birmingham. Here we had to change stations. It was now about 1 o'clock and Pat was beginning to sound very hungry and we had no food available for her, so I went along to a buffet with an empty bottle, and very kindly they filled it up with warm milk for me. Then we caught the train from Birmingham to Stratford. We occupied a first class compartment to ourselves, laid the baby in the cot on one side and Maisie hung napkins along the luggage racks to air. Then along came a ticket inspector – we had no tickets. He laughingly said that we appeared to be making ourselves at home and proceeded to the next compartment. The air gunner brevet had done the trick once again.

We arrived at Stratford about 9 o'clock after a very long day. We approached a taxi driver and asked him if he would take us up to the farm at Atherstone-on-the-Hill. He said the snow was so bad that he could take us to the bottom of the hill, but he could not get any further. When we got out of the taxi, we had a mile walk up this hill, through six or nine inches of snow and eventually we arrived at the farm house about 11 o'clock in the evening. Mrs Stoppard, who let us the rooms, was still up waiting for us and had lit a big log fire in our lounge. Living conditions here were very basic. We had no electricity and no gas, and there was no running water, so as a consequence we had oil stoves to cook by and our supply of water was got by going to the pump. The toilet was an earth one down the bottom of the garden. But in spite of this, we were very happy here. It emphasised to me that when a couple get on so well together, they can tolerate almost any conditions in order to stay with each other and live together.

We got on well with Mrs Stoppard. I do not know what had happened to my car, but we had two bikes and when the snow had cleared often Mrs Stoppard would baby-sit for us and we would cycle into Stratford to meet several of the boys and have a good drink.

Jock, Mac and I had all done a tour of operations. We had had many shaky do's and we knew that in six or nine months time, we would be back to do another thirty. We had therefore become quite war-hardened villains. Mac also lived out with his wife and we stole many things to make our lives easier. Some of the accommodations were very sparsely furnished, so we would steal blankets and sheets from the camp, anything to improve our lifestyle, not from choice, but from necessity. One evening several of us went into the lounge of a hotel in Stratford. Near closing time and after several pints Mac picked up an armchair, politely asked someone to open the door and calmly walked off with it.

Cigarettes were very scarce indeed and often it would be a question of lining up for half an hour in a queue to buy five, so sometimes when a crew became proficient and were sent off on their own, we would go along to their billets and take a carton of their cigarettes. It seemed to be justified by the fact that we had practically none, while they were Canadians who were well provided for. In addition to receiving the same meagre cigarette ration as ourselves, they got hundreds sent by their parents and friends in Canada.

As I previously mentioned, there were very many crews killed on Operational Training Units, so Jock and I made a list of Canadians who had been killed. Periodically outside the post office there appeared a list of names for whom food parcels had arrived from Canada. Jock and I would look down this list and when the names corresponded with people who had been killed, we went into the post office and told the official we were collecting the parcels on behalf of the intended recipient. After all, somebody would eventually get them. We would then cycle back to the farm and excitedly open the parcels, which contained tinned meat, chocolates and other items that were very hard to come by, in fact non-existent in England at that time.

I did my first flight on 25 January, over five hours at night across the North Sea and returning to bomb an imaginary target. I was flying regularly as an Instructor, both during the daytime and on long night cross-countries. Gradually the weather improved and Maisie and I were able to go for country walks and also cycle rides. There was the occasional mess dance which we would go to. On one occasion we cycled down from the farm to the mess for a dance. On the way there was a gate, which we had to open to cycle through. I went ahead and opened it for Maisie to come through and got on my bike not realising the gate had closed itself. Maisie went into it doing about twenty miles an hour. The bike stopped short and she went over the top of the gate. However we carried on to the dance and had a very good evening.

Pat was now eight months and crawling all over the place. In addition to milk, she was now on Farex, a cereal, and a government issue of orange juice and cod liver oil capsules, which were issued to all young children. In these days children were not over-fed and certainly it was a healthy diet.

Sometimes, I would go into town with Jock and Mac and other instructors and that was when things went a bit wrong. We would drink too much, then there would be a perilous cycle ride home without lights, and many a night when I arrived home Maisie would hold my head over a bucket while I was violently sick.

Pilot Officer Warnock was also on this OTU having

been promoted from sergeant. He was the pilot whom I had flown with at Driffield on his thirtieth operation. On 8 April however he was involved in a crash and he was killed along with three others. It was very unfortunate that a man who had survived so many operations, should have been killed in a flying accident.

Recently there appeared a request in a 104 Squadron newsletter for information about P/O Warnock by anyone who knew him or flew with him. The request was from his younger brother who lived in New Zealand to whom I replied. I received a letter from him saying he was coming to England for a holiday and would like to meet up with me.

He visited our house and we had a long and interesting conversation about David, his brother. He had been nicknamed Doc Warnock, because whenever he went away for a weekend or on leave he took a black overnight bag, similar to what doctors used. I brought out my flying log book. I was surprised to see that I had flown regularly with David, several times as his wireless operator just before his death, the last time three days previously. Why I was not crewed up on his last fateful flight I don't know. Just another piece of luck.

His brother brought a photo of him; it was exactly as I recalled him, what memories it brought back. He left it with me and it now hangs in our breakfast room.

From the farm where we were living we could look down onto the airfield and get a very good view of it. On 25 May we were out in the garden looking down at the airfield and there was a Wellington stationary, waiting for another Wellington to come in to land before turning in itself and taking off. Unfortunately, the second Wellington veered off course and crashed into the waiting one. Both aircraft went up in flames and there were twelve killed including two instructors.

The next day we were all confined to camp and the rumour had it that there was something really big going to proceed. No-one was allowed out of camp or to use a phone and on 27 May, we heard that all our aircraft at the OTU were going to go on a bombing operation, which was unusual. Sir Arthur Harris had become Commander-in-Chief of Bomber Command in February 1942. He was nicknamed 'Butch' somewhat humorously by aircrew, because of the number he sent to their doom. He flatly refused to order raids on strategic targets, but insisted that by indiscriminate bombing of German towns by sufficient aircraft he could bomb Germany into submission without opening a second front. He was proved wrong, and his stubbornness prolonged the length of the war and added to the toll of missing aircrew.

Sir Arthur Harris has always been the subject of much controversy. Some experts see him as an obstinate pig-headed man, others as a man loved and revered by air-crew. Harris spent all his time at Headquarters; he never visited any squadrons, or made any personal contact with the men he commanded. To the majority of NCO aircrew he could well have been some mythical figurehead, giving orders that were sometimes ill-judged and sometimes considered immoral. I am sure many airmen would not even have been able to name him, and very few would have revered him. He was undoubtedly arrogant. One day he was stopped for speeding and the policeman remarked,

'You might have killed someone.' To which Harris replied, 'Young man, I kill thousands of people every night.'

In furtherance of his policy Harris had decided to mount a raid with over 1,000 aircraft, and this was why OTU aircraft were being included. He had to scrape the bottom of the barrel to obtain the magic number. It was planned not only to do severe damage to a town, but also as a good propaganda exercise. It would be a wonderful boost for the morale of people in England who were still suffering very badly from German bombing attacks. The code name for this operation was Millennium and it was also intended to impress an American audience. The city was to be attacked in waves going in at three-minute intervals, with radar equipped aircraft going in front to light up the old part of Cologne with incendiary bombs. This was to act as the aiming point for the main force, when it was hoped to saturate the defences by all the bombing taking place within ninety minutes.

When the crew lists were put up I considered myself very fortunate not to be included. Our aircraft were old and obsolete and it was generally thought that they would be sitting targets for the German defences. However my good fortune was very short-lived. My very good friend Juggins had been crewed up with five Canadians who had not yet passed out. He decided that he was going to refuse to fly as he thought that after surviving so long he did not want to get killed with a crew who were not very proficient. To my dismay I was substituted. I went along to briefing and met my crew for the first time. They were obviously very inexperienced. The captain was P/O Lowe.

The briefing took place in the afternoon, and we waited

expectantly for the arrival of the CO. As usual we jumped to attention when he entered, then the usual, 'All right, men, be seated.' The large map of Europe was on the wall and in due course the ribbon was stretched to mark Cologne as the target. When the number of aircraft taking part was announced there was a gasp of astonishment, especially as the raid was to be condensed into a relatively short space of time. The risk of collision was discussed, and the Intelligence Officer said that it was projected that only two would be lost in this way. One wag shouted out, 'Yes, but which two?' A collision in the air was dreaded by all aircrew, as seldom were there any survivors.

Later there was much to do as we drew our parachutes, put on our flying clothes, and took our flasks of hot coffee, a bar of chocolate, and Horlicks tablets. This was going to be a hard time for many aircrew who had never been on operations before, and in fact had not finished their training. There was not the usual amount of banter, the atmosphere was more serious. Not being at all familiar with my crew I felt rather an outsider. But gradually we relaxed, as they were anxious to learn as much as possible from me.

We took off at twenty minutes to midnight, flew across the North Sea and arrived in the vicinity of Cologne which was the target. I plugged into the intercom and although I could hear shrapnel hitting the side of the aircraft there was no conversation going on between the crew. The rear gunner was not giving the pilot any instructions as to where the anti-aircraft was coming from and so forth, so I decided to go up into the astrodome and see what was happening for myself. We were flying along straight and level, with anti-aircraft bursting on the port side. I immediately shouted to the pilot to corkscrew to starboard, which he did, and almost immediately there was a near miss on the port side where we had been a couple of seconds previously. I shouted to him and to the bomber aimer to drop the bombs and let's get out of it as quickly as we could. We were over the town and there was no point in hanging about, especially flying straight and level, which was a sure recipe for disaster.

We were flying much slower and lower than the four-engined aircraft above us, and were attracting most of the ack-ack. Suddenly you would hear a big rumble overhead, be rocked about by an airstream and see four engines just missing you; it was very stressful. There was also the danger of being hit by bombs being released by the aircraft above.

When we left the target area I went back to my wireless, plugged in and found that it was completely dead. I did not know for what reason. Now I realised that I would not be able to give the crew any assistance with courses to fly and I hoped that the navigator was sufficiently proficient to get us back home again. Actually things went well. We landed back just after 5 o'clock in the morning. We were debriefed and then went along to the mess to have the usual egg and bacon breakfast with two or three cups of sweet tea, and always a couple of cigarettes afterwards, while you chatted away and revelled in the fact that you had completed another trip, you had survived and everything had gone well.

Our OTU had sent off 35 aircraft. Two had returned because of faults, and of the other 33 there were only four missing. In actual fact, out of the thousand aircraft that went, there were 41 missing and 230 airmen lost, which was considered very acceptable. The OTUs had been forecasted obviously to have the most percentage losses of any, but in actual fact their percentage was not much different. Out of 368 OTU aircraft, only 17 were lost, so the forecast of 'sprog crews getting the chop' was completely wrong.

The raid caused considerable excitement to the British public. *The Times* proclaimed, '1000 **BOMBERS RAID COLOGNE.** Biggest air attack of the war. 2000 tons of Bombs in 40 minutes.' And it was good, encouraging news for the general public.

The following afternoon I went out to the aircraft that I had flown in to see what had caused the problem with the wireless. The wireless mechanic was taking the set out. He said to me, 'Where were you last night?'

I said, 'Sitting here by the radio.'

He said, 'You weren't when this came in,' and he produced a piece of shrapnel that had gone through the aircraft where I usually sat and into the radio, but obviously it had occurred when I was supervising at the astrodome. If I had been sitting there the wireless set would have been working perfectly, but I would not have been. He gave me the piece of shrapnel. It measured about 3 inches by 2 inches and had a thread on the inside. I kept it for many years, but now apparently it has been mislaid.

The raid was a great success in terms of achieving its purpose, as visualised by 'Butch' Harris, our supreme commander, but many people, including aircrew, viewed with dismay such indiscriminate bombing of civilians.

Germany had done the same thing on a smaller scale, but that was no valid reason to lower our moral standards. The German version of events which came to light after the war stated:

> Within 90 minutes the centre of the city lay in ruins, with 460 dead, 45,000 homeless, 3,300 houses and 36 industrial buildings totally destroyed, and a further 20% of all buildings in the town damaged.

And about 150,000 fled from the town immediately to become refugees in other parts of Germany.

Juggins, whom I had replaced, was never seen again. He had been found guilty of LMF, that is, 'lack of moral fibre' (cowardice), and the punishment for this was that he would be stripped of his Flight-Sergeant's stripes and crown and sent to another station. The marks where his Sergeant's stripes had been removed would be perfectly obvious and everybody would know what had happened to him. Besides this, he would have no trade and as a consequence would be given all the menial tasks of an air force station, such as washing up and cleaning out latrines. Once you got LMF on your records you were finished, no promotion, you were not wanted by the powers that be. And this was a man who had already completed at least thirty operations and nearly six months as an instructor under difficult conditions. It was quite a severe punishment for somebody who, just on one occasion, had refused to fly. And he would have been quite happy to have been posted to an operational squadron as part of an experienced crew. But LMF was never a great problem. Although most crews of Bomber Command fought an unending battle with fear, few succumbed and refused to fly.

The Canadian pupils on this OTU were mad on playing crap, that is dice, so always there would be two or three dice schools going on when we were not flying. I was an inveterate gambler and always took part in these sessions. There is no skill about this game but I always seemed to have more than my share of luck. For the uninitiated, crap is played with two dice, both numbered 1 to 6. The thrower makes a money bet, i.e. he puts into the bank the amount of money he wishes to wager, which is covered by one or more of the other players. If his first throw totals 7 or 11 he wins, but if he throws 2, 3 or 12 he loses. In any of these cases, he bets and throws again. If his throw totals 4, 5, 6, 8, 9 or 10, that number becomes his point and he continues to throw until he makes the same point again or throws a 7. If he makes his point he wins, but if he throws a 7 he loses both his bet and the right to throw again, and the dice are passed to the next player. There are also side bets made, but these are rather complicated to explain.

One evening we started playing, waiting for flying, and a Canadian had lost all his money while I was well in pocket. He said, 'I'll throw anybody my car for £25.' I took him up on this. He took the dice and threw 10, one of the more difficult numbers to throw again, as there are only 3 combinations of that number, whereas 7 has six combinations. And fortunately for me he eventually threw a 7 and I had won his pride and joy. The next morning I went home to Maisie with a very nice little Austin 7 sports car. It was a two-seater with a rounded back that could be opened up as a dickie seat in which another person could sit. We had many enjoyable outings in it. I never taxed or insured it, little things like that did not bother us. Although this was the only way to obtain petrol coupons, we always seemed to manage somehow to fiddle enough for our requirements. One day I went over a level crossing too fast, the car jumped into the air, banged down again, and the dickie seat dropped off and was left behind. I wonder whatever happened to that lovely Austin 7?

A further 1,000 raid (actually 956 aircraft took part) was mounted against Essen on 30 May. Luckily I was not crewed up, as the raid was a complete failure owing to bad weather and wrongly forecasted winds. German radio did not even recognise Essen as the target and reported 'widespread raids over Western Germany'. The loss was 31 aircraft and 212 airmen.

I carried on with my normal instruction duties until 25 June when another 1,000 bomber operation was mounted against Bremen. I flew this time with an experienced pilot, Flight Sergeant Clayton, whom I had known previously on 102 Squadron. But the rest of the crew were novices and we were flying in an aircraft only fit for training exercises. Once again the met. forecasts were wrong. Instead of clear skies Bremen was blanketed in cloud. This necessitated us flying around for a while trying to identify the Deschimag shipyard, which was our target: unpleasant when the anti-aircraft was rattling around us. Eventually we dropped our bombs and had an uneventful return home. This was the most costly 1,000 bomber raid, as 50 were missing and 65 were seriously damaged of which 22 had to be scrapped. The casualty rate amongst instructors was catastrophic (40 per cent). Our OTU fared rather better; we only lost two out of ten sent. The three 1,000 bomber raids had cost 122 aircraft missing, and many more seriously damaged and written off. No more took place until near the end of the war.

The OTU was still losing aircraft in training, either in crashes or going completely missing when doing long flights on a triangular course over the North Sea. Since I had joined the OTU fifteen aircraft and crews had been lost. Small things often caused accidents to the inexperienced. For instance the pitot head is a small device which gives the airspeed on the instrument panel inside the aircraft. It is a pipe, situated outside the aircraft; and on the ground it is protected by a cotton bag which is removed before take-off. Sometimes in flight a bird will get caught in it and cause an obstruction, or the cotton bag will fail to be removed. In such cases the pilot has no knowledge of his airspeed. One such incident occurred when the pilot announced over the radio that his airspeed indicator had failed and that he was coming in to land. He obviously came in too slowly and with a further message, 'Christ, we've had it,' he spun into the ground. All six were killed.

I had the same thing happen on two occasions when flying with experienced pilots, but both came in to make a perfect landing. They could tell by the feel of the aircraft and the noise of the wind the exact speed at which we were travelling.

Maisie and I were continuing to enjoy life at the farm. Pat had her first birthday, was walking, and looked very well and happy. I managed to borrow a rifle with which we used to shoot the odd rabbit or pigeon in order to supplement our diet. One summer evening I shot two pigeons which I put in a corner in the living room. It was a lovely warm evening and Maisie and I went for a long walk through the countryside. When we returned we found the pigeons had disappeared, a trail of feathers indicating that cats had been the culprits.

One day a notice appeared on the board saying that any wireless operator who had completed over thirty operations could apply to be considered for training as a Signals Officer. On reading this I was terribly excited. A 'Signals Officer'; it would put a stop to any further operational flying and I was approaching the time when I would be called upon to do another tour, this time probably with a Pathfinder Squadron. My starting money as an officer would be twice as much as I was getting. I applied and duly passed the selection board and it was wonderful news for both of us because it meant that at no time in the future, theoretically, would I have to put my neck on the chopping block. In due course Maisie packed up and went back to London to share her time between her mother and my mother and father. I proceeded to go to Cranwell to be trained as a Signals Officer.

Maisie, Pat and I had enjoyed a very pleasant nine months at Atherstone. Mrs Stoppard had been very easy to get on with. We had made use of the good weather to have long walks and picnics etc., and many pleasant evenings were spent in good company. The break was not too bad as Jock Cullen, Jack Young and others of my friends had recently been posted to the North African Desert to operate against Rommel and the German army. I probably would have gone as well had I not applied to become a Signals Officer.

In May 1992, out of interest, I went to a trade show organised by Crown Wallpapers and we were accommodated for two days in a luxurious hotel in Stratford. I took the opportunity to visit the cottage where we had lived so happily. There it was, exactly the same as fifty years earlier, except that water and electricity had been laid on and the outside pump had been stolen, I was informed, on the day that the owner died. And I visited the airfield on the very same day that fifty years before I had taken off on the 1,000 bomber raid to Cologne. Nostalgia? Buckets of it.

Chapter Thirteen

ABOUT THREE WEEKS after arriving at Cranwell I dropped myself into serious trouble. One Saturday morning, feeling very much in need of female company, I decided to see if I could get a pass to go home to Maisie for the weekend. There was nobody in the orderly room and I saw the pass forms tantalisingly on the table in front of me. I moved forward, tore one off, stamped it, forged the CO's signature, and inserted the date. Off I went in high spirits.

Apparently the railways had had a lot of trouble that day from air raids and as a consequence I was not able to catch a train until midnight. When I got out at London, around 5 or 6 o'clock in the morning, I was about the only serviceman to alight. A Corporal SP immediately came up to me and asked to see my pass. I gave it to him. I do not know what was wrong with it, probably I might have put the wrong date, but he asked me to accompany him to his office. He then phoned Cranwell and found out that I did not have a pass at all. He said to me, 'I can't order you to go back, but I would strongly advise you to do so.' I realised that I was in a bit of a jam and it did not seem to me to make much difference whether I went straight back or later on that day. So I decided after all to go home to Maisie.

We had a few drinks midday, a nice Sunday lunch, and couple of hours in bed in the afternoon, and about 6 o'clock in the evening I caught the train back to Grantham. At least I should have got out at Grantham. However, having been up all the night before and having had a strenuous Sunday, I fell asleep and I did not wake up until I found myself in Scotland. So the only thing I could do was take a train back to Grantham and hope for the best. I arrived back into the camp about 4 o'clock Monday afternoon, wishing I had taken the advice of the Corporal SP and returned straight back to camp. I met one or two of my colleagues on the course coming out of the guardroom and they confirmed that I was in the dog-house. When I went into the guardroom I was immediately put under arrest for being absent without leave, and also for other serious charges, including forgery.

A couple of days afterwards I had a committee of inquiry which is a prelude to a court-martial. I was defended by an officer with legal qualifications. I still have the written advice he gave me. He instructed me to make the following statement:

> On September 27th, 1942, as is the case on each Sunday of the course, I was not detailed for attendance at any lectures.
>
> Considering, therefore, that I was free for the entire day, I resolved to journey to London to see my wife who had communicated with me in a letter which I received the previous Saturday. The nature of this letter was such that I sought the first opportunity of visiting her.

I thought that owing to the short time available I might not be able to secure an official pass, so I decided to travel without one.

At Grantham Station I was asked to produce a F295 (leave pass) for the purpose of obtaining a cheap fare and accordingly I signed a F295 which I later produced at King Cross Station on being questioned by the RAF Service Police.

He also listed several questions he would ask me and the replies I should make.

During this period of trouble Maisie was very worried indeed, which was obvious from the letters she wrote to me. One was as follows:

I know what a terrible blow it will be for you if they take you off the course. Perhaps good luck will be on our side, anyway we must look on the bright side whatever turns up and remember that the war can't go on forever.

I do so want to cheer you up, I do feel that you really need me and I would give anything to put things back where they were. It made my heart ache to see you so unhappy on Sunday, but whatever happens I love you and we have our Pat. So don't do anything rash, will you, dear.

And later Maisie wrote:

My dearest,

Things certainly look very bad for us, I don't suppose that there is any chance of your staying on the course now, is there! if only they would give you a chance, There must be heeps of boys doing what you did, you must be one of the unlucky ones, or perhaps it was ment to happen for some reason we dont know of. It just seems so hard after all you have gone through to get where you are. One thing dear, if you are stripped we wont have the worry we had last year & w. can manage on the money if we go easy, so long as I have you I dont mind."

Such letters from Maisie gave me consolation and comfort. But our worries soon ceased; the old Mourton luck emerged again.

After another couple of days I was told to report to the CO and when I got in front on him he said to me, 'You are very fortunate indeed, Mourton. We are short of courts-martial and therefore I have been told to give you a severe reprimand,' which he proceeded to do. I was freed from arrest and carried on with the course.

A Signals Officer was responsible for all means of communication on an airfield or aircraft. It was his responsibility for telephones, teleprinter, receiving stations, transmitting stations, right down to carrier pigeons, if there were any housed on the station. The course was a nineteen-week intensive one, mainly dealing with theory and procedure. I was very interested in the actual practical operation of receiving and transmitting radio messages, but I had very little interest in the theory of it.

Discipline was very lax here, and Barney, with whom I had become very friendly, and I both had bicycles, and we would cycle around the countryside buying up eggs, butter, whatever we could, to take home the following weekend. We spent every evening out drinking and as a consequence, we paid very little interest in the course that was proceeding. Our philosophy was that we would make it all up later on, it would be all right on the day. However, when we got to about two weeks from the final examination, we knew that our knowledge was very limited. Every evening there was a class for those people who wanted extra tuition, so we decided to go along to this and make up for lost time.

I had the ability and intelligence to pick things up, but I am afraid I lacked the enthusiasm and interest, and as a consequence, my knowledge of the course was negligible. The evening before the final examination we went along as usual for the extra tuition and at the end of the lesson the Chief Instructor lifted some papers up and said, 'This is the examination paper which you are going to face tomorrow,' and as a joke he added, 'I expect you would all like to have a look at it.' With that he put it away in a drawer, we filed out, and he locked the hut up.

We were both certain now that we were doomed to failure next day and suddenly the possibility, or reality, of going back to a squadron and having to complete thirty more operations became imminent. One of us said, 'That exam paper, I wonder if we could get into the hut and get hold of it.' So we turned round and went back to the hut. We went round the back. Barney had a penknife which he used to open the top window, then he put his hand inside, opened the main casement window and we entered. The black-out was very efficient, so we were able to turn the lights on. We had our note-books and pencils, and we proceeded to copy out all the questions into our note-books. Even with our knowledge of the questions our information was so limited, we did not know the answers. We went back to our hut and everyone there was sitting on their beds busily swotting up for the next day. So I went round to one or two of them and said, 'Just assume the following question was asked tomorrow, how would you answer it?' and then I would relate one of the questions that was on the examination paper. By this method I was able to make some notes and later on sit on the bed memorising as much as I could. In addition, I was also able to make a few very small abbreviations on a piece of paper.

Next day, when I went in for the examination, I found it comparatively easy with the knowledge I had acquired the evening before and the piece of paper that went unnoticed by the examiner. I easily passed the examination but to my horror I found that there was to be an oral examination conducted by the Chief Instructor. When I went in front of him I found it impossible to answer the questions he was giving me. He said, 'I can't understand it, Mourton. You did a very good written paper, but now your knowledge seems almost negligible.' I managed to persuade him that I had the knowledge but was shy and embarrassed in front of him. He accepted this explanation and in due course I passed. Poor old Barney failed and I do not know what happened to him.

It was about this time that I had a letter from Jock Cullum, with whom Maisie and I had been so friendly during our nine months at Atherstone. There was a long delay in receiving it, as it came from North Africa and was sent to my home, addressed incorrectly to Streatham, instead of Tooting. The following is the letter as I received it.

4 the Aug. 1942   F/Sgt W. Cullen
                              970943.
                 242 Wing RAF
                      M.E.F.
              c/o No 8 Ward
My Dear Dougie.   No 12 Gen. Hosp.

another   no doubt you are having
if I am   look   at my address to see
really in hospital. Yep!
They got me at last. It's a long story
as you can guess from when y'
last saw you till now but briefly
here you are. Still with Sharpe
we got out successfully & got onto
our trips. about the 10th we
ran out of petrol coming back from
Tobruk & force landed. We were
unlucky. Only Bill Stanbury &
myself were the only ones worth
picking out of the wreckage &
he snuffed it the next night:
Yours truly has been U/S for a
couple of months but. I am.
happy to say is nearly on his

feet again. Knowing me as you do you appreciate I have a few tales to spin you, but space is not what it used to be, so they will have to wait till that happy day when we can swap yarns

Lying in bed two days ago feeling cheesed off to hell a tall familiar figure walked towards my bed — Ye Gods etc it was Jock Young !!! Was I happy! We only had a brief chat in which I was very glad to find you were still going strong etc. I can hardly wait to see him again as you can guess, must pack up now (my right hand had a couple of broken bones & it's not up to scratch yet anyway) Need I say that memories of our friendship have been an inspiration to me in good times & in bad. I trust that it will not be too long before we can have a pint together again. My kindest regards to your

150

folks & as to Maisie — well I reckon this letter is as much hers as yours so I'll say "Hello Maisie" — hope you & the baby are well.

Kindest wishes & all good fortune to you from Jock Cullen

It illustrates the flippant way in which casualties were regarded. It also shows the very deep friendship that had existed between Jock and myself. That was the last letter I had from him. I heard later on that he had once again been the sole survivor in a crash. You could not be more lucky than that. Jock survived the war, he called at my parents' house shortly after the end of the war, but unfortunately no details of his whereabouts were given and I have not been able to trace him.

Having passed the course at Cranwell, there was only one obstacle now left. Before being commissioned we moved to Cosford for a month's course where they endeavoured to pass you out, not only as an officer, but also a gentleman. I thought it was a waste of time, especially with the war entering a critical stage. It was at Cosford that we saw a most remarkable happening: an aircraft moving down the runway and taking off – without engines or propellers. We were astounded, not knowing that it was the first jet propelled aircraft having its trials.

In due course, our instruction completed, I passed out as Pilot Officer Mourton. I received a grant of £50 to buy my uniform and other necessities for an officer. I went down to Burberry's in London, a very well known and respected outfitters, and I was able to buy two perfectly fitting barathea uniforms, made to measure, a crombie greatcoat, shirts, ties, socks, shoes and other ancillary equipment such as an officer's bed, and I still had change left out of the £50. I also had fifteen days' leave and I went home feeling rather proud, especially as I walked along and acknowledged the salutes of airmen and soldiers, although sometimes feeling embarrassed.

F/Lt Douglas Mourton on qualification as a Signals Officer.

Chapter Fourteen

M Y FIRST POSTING as an officer was to Stradishall. This was a parent station of two other airfields and my duty was Assistant Signals Officer. I was not at all comfortable here. I did not like the work and certainly I did not like living in the officers mess, which was so different to the sergeants mess where I had been living for several years. The atmosphere was different. I knew no-one and I felt out of it.

This was the time when I started to have trouble with my nerves. I could not integrate with life in the officers mess, and as a consequence I would go for long walks by myself in the evening before retiring to bed to have quite a sleepless night. At breakfast the next morning I would sit by myself, then if other people happened to sit down opposite me I felt so embarrassed I would get up and leave my meal.

It therefore became urgent that I found living out accommodation, in order that I could be joined by Maisie and Pat. Eventually, I found a vicarage that offered us two rooms which were free in exchange for Maisie doing the cooking. It was in a very pretty little village, Cavendish in

Suffolk. Pat was now walking quite well, and we would go for walks, chatting with the villagers and feeling very satisfied with our life. The vicar had a daughter and often she and her friends would enter the church, and then we would hear jazz music emanating from the organ. The vicarage possessed a tennis court, where often several of us would compete, followed by afternoon tea. Life went on here just as it did in peace-time, no bombs, no difference at all except for rationing, but in the country this could be easily supplemented. We were only here for a few weeks, for what reason I cannot recall; but then we moved to a very nice house at Clare in Suffolk, where the same arrangement took place for Maisie to do the cooking in exchange for the accommodation. I was cycling back and forth from Stradishall every day.

I was still having problems with my nerves. Some evenings when Maisie and I went out for a drink and other people sat near us, and probably entered into conversation, I would feel most embarrassed and have to ask Maisie to leave the pub with me. I was also having peculiar tremors that were running up my back into my head, giving me the impression that something terrible was going to happen immediately. This had first happened to me years previously after I had baled out on my second operation, but gradually then things had got better. I think it was the result of the hours of hypertension I had spent operating over Germany for two years. Apart from this, things were going very smoothly, but I still felt out of place at Stradishall and was not enjoying work at all and I could not wait every evening to get on my bike and cycle back home to Maisie.

After two or three months at Stradishall I was very pleased indeed to receive a posting to RAF Newmarket, where I thought things must be better than they were at Stradishall. Here I was the Station Signals Officer and as a consequence received promotion to Flight Lieutenant. I was in charge of everything on the station from a signals point of view.

It was now that I fully realised my shortcomings as a Signals Officer. But very fortunately I had as my next in command a Warrant Officer Street, who was a peace time signals operator who knew the job absolutely inside out. I got on very well with him; I had to. He was greatly indebted to me soon after I arrived. He had been happily living out with his wife, when a bombshell arrived in the form of a posting to the Far East. I compiled a letter to the relevant authority asking for the posting to be cancelled owing to the ill health of his wife (she was perfectly hale and hearty). It worked. I was relying on him so much, I did not want to lose him. He organised everything and I became merely a figure-head who signed papers and did as I was told. In contrast to Stradishall I felt very much at home at Newmarket. Everyone seemed very friendly and I felt that my posting had been a great improvement.

There were two clubs in Newmarket that were open to officers and one in particular, the Craven Club, I would visit regularly in the evening, drinking and playing cards with three other officers. I was an extremely good solo player, and as a consequence I won a fair amount of money.

Newmarket was the home of the British horse racing industry and as a consequence it was also the home of gambling. One evening Walter Earl, a race horse trainer, came to the mess and said that his filly, Garden Path, would win the St Leger without any doubt. Apparently it was unusual for a filly to run against colts in this particular race, but we took his word for it and between us in the officers mess we collected £60 to wager on this horse. It was put on at an ante-post price of 10 to 1. Harry Wragg, the jockey, rode this horse; it was backed down to favourite at 9 to 2 and it won in a canter. So the officers who had participated in the flutter collected between us £660 that evening and, as you can imagine, a very good party took place. One evening at the Craven Club I met a professional gambler and we arranged to go to the race meeting next day together, when he would give me some good information. It turned out very different to what I expected. He made four wagers of £250, and the horses all lost. Unfortunately I also backed them.

I had to find living accommodation for Maisie and Pat, and someone recommended me to try the vicarage at Gazeley which was six or seven miles out of Newmarket. As soon as possible I met Maisie one morning and we went to Newmarket and decided to have lunch at a pub in the centre of the town. It was here that we saw a very attractive blonde walk in and have a drink with a companion. Later on when we got to the vicarage at Gazeley and knocked at the door it was answered by this very blonde that we had seen in the pub. She was the vicar's wife. She was a Dane who had come to England to recruit members to be Jehovah's Witnesses. But she had altered her mind when she met a vicar and in due course married him.

We had a very happy time at Newmarket. Once again we were given two rooms in exchange for Maisie doing the cooking for the family. Every evening we would go to the pub and meet a contingent of soldiers who had returned from fighting in North Africa. One of them played a ukulele and most evenings we had a sing-song, with three or four pints of bitter, and would go to bed thoroughly happy. Whatever happened to the Austin 7 I won, I really do not know. These possessions in wartime seemed to come and go and nobody seemed to bother very much about it. I had a bike and this I was riding backwards and forwards each day between Gazeley and Newmarket.

I attended my first mess meeting and this was presided over by the Camp Commander, Group Captain Sharp. He asked during the course of the meeting whether anyone knew anything about decorating. Pre-war, as a representative, I had been selling wallpapers and paint and other decorating items and consequently I put my hand up. It is an unwritten law in the services never to volunteer for anything under any circumstances and what induced me to put my hand up I really do not know, but I paid very dearly for it.

'Good,' said Group Captain Sharp, 'in that case, Mourton, you can be in charge of decorating the interior of the officers mess. Owing to the shortage of labour nowadays there are no contractors available and everything has to be done on a self help basis. You will acquire what decorating materials you require and you will be provided with the labour to carry the work out.'

In 1943, after four years of war, it was virtually impossible to buy any decorating materials. However, I contacted Hadfield's, paint manufacturers of Mitcham, with whom I had had good contact before the war and they agreed to send me a quantity of paint along. This turned out to be orange gloss. At this particular time the only paint that was ever used was various shades of cream, green and brown, nothing else was ever seen. That was probably why this orange paint had been sitting on the shelves since before the war.

The labour that I was given was airmen on jankers. Jankers was a form of punishment for various crimes that had been committed. A man on jankers would do his normal day's work and then report to the guard-room in full kit; and this had to be really first class. After that he would be allocated various menial tasks for the next two or three hours, and a half dozen of these janker wallahs were sent to me each evening to do their two or three hour stint. You can imagine that they were not terribly enthusiastic about decorating the officers mess.

Eventually the work was finished, everything in orange paint, the dining hall, the lounge, the corridors, the toilets, orange wherever you went. It was decided to have a mess dance to celebrate. I took Maisie down to Newmarket to buy a new dress for this special occasion. We finally settled on a blue angora wool dress. I can remember it cost £13, which was a lot of money. Maisie looked very attractive in it and I felt very proud of her. It turned out an excellent evening, although I did have to withstand some ribald comments concerning the orange paint. These were all given and taken in good spirit however.

I was always ready for a game of cards and I do not know how it happened, but I got teamed up with three airmen and every morning during working hours we would retire to a room that was never used, in the totalisator building that had been commandeered by the air force. Here we would settle down for a few hours playing solo. One morning, however, the Group Captain walked in with the Station Warrant Officer. They saw four of us sitting round a table, with four heaps of coins by our sides and the air thick with cigarette smoke. The CO said, 'Take these airmen's names, and Mourton, I'll deal with you later.' It was a very serious offence for an officer to be caught playing with three airmen, especially during working hours. In due course, the dreaded summons came over the Tannoy and I presented myself at the CO's office.

I saluted smartly. Group Captain Sharp said to me, 'Mourton, you were playing cards with three airmen.'

'Yes, sir.'

'What game were you playing?'

'Solo, sir.'

'I see. You live out with your wife, don't you?' (Was my sleeping out pass going to be cancelled?)

'That's right, sir.'

'Does your wife play solo?' (What goes on here?)

'Yes, sir.'

'Well, do you know, Mourton, my wife and I love a game of solo and we can never find anyone to play with. Will you and your wife come down to our cottage next Friday evening and have a meal and an evening's solo with us?'

'Certainly, sir.'

What a fantastic piece of luck. I had imagined all sorts of horrible punishments and instead of that we were going to spend a very nice evening with the Group Captain and his wife. In fact it became a regular occurrence. And not only did we have a good meal there, but most evenings we took their money as well. I became very good friends with the CO; we often discussed the race meetings and regularly he would ask me to place bets for him.

Even during the war, horse racing took place quite frequently on the Newmarket race-course, and most racing days I would take the day off and Maisie and I would go down there. Usually we would go on my bike with Maisie on the cross bar. Sometimes we won, sometimes we were forced to borrow money to pay back on the next pay-day. I remember Maisie queuing up for quite a while in the rain to draw 2s.3d. she had won on the last race. We still did not look to any future at all. It was just a question of living from hand to mouth from day to day, hoping for the best.

Rev. Humphries was the vicar with whom we were living. He was the vicar of Gazeley and the rector of Dalham, a nearby village, so he had two livings. Often on a Sunday morning he would walk into the church about 10.50 am, ring the bells a few times and then return at 11.10 because nobody had turned up. He never did any visiting; he was a very poor churchman. Also part-time he worked at Cambridge University translating old Latin documents. His wife was charming, but he adopted a superior air and was also an alcoholic. He was often assisted home from the local pub, which was only a short distance away.

Somehow I acquired another car, an old Morris 8, well dented but still capable of small journeys. Sometimes Rev. Humphries would phone me up at the airfield and ask me to meet him at the off-licence on my way home. The object was for me to pick up a barrel of beer – my reward was the first pint drawn off, very thick and cloudy. Then he could be seen half hidden in the kitchen, having his first pint about 8.30 am each morning.

There were three boys in the family, seven, five and three years old. I have always got on well with children, making up stories, doing tricks and playing games. These three enjoyed my company and I spent a lot of time with them in the evenings; I felt sorry for them, as they did not have much of a life and one was a cripple from birth. I would perform simple conjuring tricks and make up the most unlikely stories. This really annoyed Humphries and he would order me out, but I would be back again next evening.

In the early part of 1944, I went back to flying again with Bomber Development Unit, which was based at Newmarket. It was interesting as BDU were developing radar aids, which at this stage of the war were very sophisticated. We would invent something which gave our bomber force a good advantage, the Germans would invent something to counteract it, and so the tussle would go on. Probably because Group Captain Sharp was CO and a most tolerant and easy-going man, Newmarket was a delightful station on which to be serving. Discipline was lax; it was very free and easy. When my brother visited us, and also Maisie's brother, they were able to visit the airfield and have trips in a Lancaster bomber that I had arranged. It was always easy to get time off; Maisie and I never missed a race meeting.

One day I was Duty Officer, which meant I had to be on

call for twenty-four hours in the mess. That evening I sat beside a group playing poker. I had never come across this game before, but after a couple of hours I had a good knowledge of it by watching the play and learning the rules. The next afternoon I went down to the Craven Club because I had backed two horses and they got the results through on the phone immediately the races were over. Sitting at a table were four individuals with a pack of cards.

'Want to make up a five for poker?' said one.

Rather hesitantly I agreed. The betting seemed fairly steep and I won the first hand and gained £20. The next hand I threw in, and I was then transfixed by the amounts two were betting against each other. At the end of the hand the pool was over £200. How could I get out of this situation, especially as I was winning? Then a steward came over and asked if I was F/Lt. Mourton; I was wanted on the phone. I had told the operator where I was going, if I was required. It was only some small problem, but it enabled me to go back to the card table and tell them I was wanted urgently back at the airfield. I vowed to be more careful in future.

It was about August 1944 that Maisie realised she was pregnant again. We were well established at the vicarage, who appreciated the cooking Maisie was doing for them; it gave Mrs Humphries a lot more time to devote to her children. We did not expect another baby would create too much of a problem. Life was very enjoyable, not too much work, and nice walks in the country, Pat was three years old and such a good child. She was a favourite with many people in the village.

And then on 30 November 1944 the bombshell

dropped. I was being posted to the Far East to the Combat Cargo Task Force. At this time Germany was retreating on all fronts, beaten, but Japan was still a force to be reckoned with. The name of the unit which I was joining sounded very belligerent. Once again I would be leaving Maisie and Pat just before Christmas, and unhappily Maisie was almost five months pregnant. We had enjoyed a very pleasant stay at Newmarket, there had been no undue strain, we had made many friends and my nerve trouble had improved.

Nine years ago Jenny, my daughter and Keith, her husband, suggested that to celebrate our Golden Wedding anniversary they would take Maisie and me for a journey down Memory Lane, visiting the airfields where I had served and the houses where we had lived. We called at the vicarage, and the door was opened by the same beautiful lady that we had first met forty-six years ago. But now, alas, time had taken its toll. She was very old, with a bent back and was only able to walk with the aid of walking sticks. When her husband had died she had reverted to being a Jehovah's Witness. Each bedroom had about a dozen mattresses laid on the floor to accommodate the people who attended the big meetings that her son, also a Jehovah's Witness, held. When she saw us she recognised us at once and tears came into her eyes. We chatted about old times and she said her sons still spoke of the stories, tricks and games that I used to entertain them with. Then we visited the two rooms where we had lived a comfortable and pleasant life and visited the old pub where we had spent so many evenings with real friends, sadly all passed on, being that bit older than us.

Chapter Fifteen

M Y POSTING WAS an urgent one, initially to Karachi, in India; no embarkation leave. I got a lift from Newmarket to Liverpool on a Lancaster and Maisie and Pat were there to see me off. At Liverpool we had several injections and were going to sail the next day. We were told not to take any alcohol after being injected. But what does a crowd of airmen do on their last day in England? We went to the nearest pub, which was some distance away from the camp, and sank a few pints. The effect was that we almost had to walk back on our hands and knees – we felt diabolical.

However, the next day I was told my posting was so urgent I was being flown out to India. I was taken down to Lineham. On 4 December 1944, on an unarmed Liberator, we travelled by a roundabout route to avoid German fighters, to El Adam in North Africa. It was a very long trip and the camp was just a few buildings in the middle of a vast desert. And airmen served a minimum of three years here, God knows how they occupied their spare time.

Early next morning we proceeded to Shaibah, another

camp in the middle of nowhere and the subject of an old RAF song, 'I've got those Shaibah blues', the words of which are not sung in decent company. There was an officers club here and in the evening four of us visited it. The only possible drink was a rough South African brandy. I do not know how many we had, but next morning I had the biggest hangover ever; I was trembling, my heart was missing beats, I was genuinely worried that I was on the way out. We had an early call and flew on 6 December to Karachi. I proceeded to a transit mess and got quite nice accommodation.

The next day I went to the Orderly Room to get instructions where to go next. Various enquiries were made, but no-one had any knowledge of why I was there, so I spent a couple of weeks in Karachi, sight-seeing. I went to two race meetings, but became very bored in the evenings. I was in an officers transit mess and people were always coming and going. In the daytime however I could go sight-seeing in a completely different world. I had never left England before. I visited the best Chinese restaurant ever, spoke to many Indians who had a limited knowledge of the English language, and went to many religious shrines. After a while an official suggested I should go to Delhi and see if they had any information there, so I caught a plane and reported to the official Orderly Room. Once again no news, no information, so I settled in to another transit mess, having to report daily to the Orderly Room.

While in India all ranks had to take a mepacrine tablet every day; it was compulsory. It prevented malaria, and consequently it was a court-martial offence if anyone contracted it. But these tablets turned the skin into a shade of pale yellow and I was worried about the side-effects they might have when taken over a long period. I never took a single one and luckily I still avoided malaria.

After I had been in Delhi about a week I was having a drink in the bar one evening and got into conversation with a Wing Commander. He told me he was flying a Dakota that night down to Ceylon, a trial run to see if it would go that far without refuelling. I knew that my brother Eric was somewhere in the vicinity of Ceylon on HMS *Wolfe*, so I asked the Wing Commander if he would give me a lift down there and he agreed. We shifted a few more beers and we took off finally at 1 am, myself bedding down in a state of inebriation in the fuselage. Obviously I would forgo my daily report to the orderly room, but I did not even think about it. That was on 23 December 1944. Delhi in December is very cold at night, usually with a frost, so I was wearing a thick uniform, overcoat and so on to keep warm. After flying for nearly eleven hours we touched down at RAF Ratmalana in Ceylon. I staggered out of the Dakota; it was sweltering, about 75 degrees and very humid. And I had no light khaki clothing, I had lost my cap and I had no money.

I went into the officers mess and posed as a Transport Command Wireless Operator awaiting a flight back to my base: I was allotted a hut with all conveniences and had my meals in the dining room. Ratmalana was a very pleasant station, situated in the middle of a vast coconut plantation, but one had to be careful, because often when walking through the trees a coconut would drop dangerously close. On looking up one would see a monkey up there, almost with a grin on his face.

For a small tip young boys would shin up a coconut tree and bring one down. When fresh the skins are quite soft and when the top is cut off a drink of delicious coconut milk is provided. The actual coconut is also quite soft.

After a few days I was able to hitch a lift into Trincomalee, the main naval base. I went into one of the naval offices, informed them my brother was serving on HMS *Wolfe* and enquired whether it was within easy reach. They were very helpful, said that it was anchored a few miles off and offered to provide a launch to take me there. Being an officer I was duly piped aboard the *Wolfe*. Someone pointed my brother out to me; he was working on a gun with his back towards me. I approached and tapped him on the shoulder. He was flabbergasted because he did not even know I had left England.

After swapping yarns, we saw his captain who agreed he could have some immediate leave. It transpired that the *Wolfe* was permanently anchored off Trincomalee, serving as a submarine refuelling and repair depot. We went back to the island, the amusing fact being that because I was an officer and my brother a rating two launches were provided for us to travel separately. My brother decided he would return to the boat each night to sleep as liberty boats were always running back and forth, but I needed to find accommodation. The only hotel was full, but it was suggested that I tried the local missionary. He was very obliging, lived in a nice bungalow and provided me with a bedroom.

And so I proceeded to have a most enjoyable week with

my brother. We swam, sunbathed and walked round the beautiful beaches and through the shady forests, which were alive with monkeys of all descriptions. We ate in local restaurants, and in the evenings we went to the naval PO's bar, where we drank very strong Australian beer, probably called Black Cat, and the rum issued by the authorities to all naval personnel, which my brother had stored rather than drunk. I had no money, but my brother had plenty because of the difficulty in spending it when permanently aboard a ship.

One evening I returned early to the bungalow, in a very happy state, singing away, unfortunately interrupting a Bible class being held by the missionary. Next morning the missionary asked me always to enter by the back entrance.

There was a rubber plantation nearby, and the local women could be seen walking with large baskets carefully balanced on their heads. They walked in lines so gracefully and seductively, pleasant to watch. All were slim, probably owing to years of exercise that their work provided, and the food they ate.

But all good things come to an end, and after a week, I decided I must return. There was quite a chance that someone had been looking for me. My brother provided me with money, not lent, we had that sort of relationship. It had been easy to get to Ceylon; it might be difficult to get back to Delhi, but once again I posed as Transport Command, and with a series of hops through Bombay, Karachi etc. I arrived back at Delhi.

Still I was not wanted, but when I visited the orderly room I received some most disturbing news from my father. Apparently when I left England Maisie had moved out from the vicarage to live with two sisters whose husbands were serving abroad, in a house quite near to the vicarage. It meant she would have more company, much better than living alone at the vicarage. But after a few days there she had got up in the night and had a miscarriage, a very serious affair, as she was over five months pregnant, and she lost a considerable amount of blood. She had lain for hours in the toilet until she was discovered next morning. She was rushed to Newmarket Hospital and put in the intensive care unit. Long afterwards I was told she had almost died, and in fact an invoice we still have from an official is addressed to 'The executors of the late Mrs. K. Mourton.'

```
                    The Executors of the Late
                         Mrs. Morton,
                       "Rosemont,"
                         GAZELEY,
                          nr. Newmarket,
                             Suffolk
```

BOOK 52.   No......43....

Name...Mrs..Morton(deceased)..................   Date...19 FEB 1945

Telephone.:   To Suffolk Branch British Red Cross Society
1154 & 5., Bury St. Edmund's.
Telegrams: THE PANELS, 10, NORTHGATE STREET,
County Director,   BURY ST. EDMUND'S.
Bury St. Edmund's.
All Communications should be
made to the County Director.   For use of Ambulance.

| 15 1 45 | Gazeley to Bury Hospital. | 9 | - |

Cheques and Postal Orders, to be crossed Lloyds Bank, Ltd.

What a traumatic experience it must have been for Maisie, to be away from her husband, her family and friends in such circumstances, and probably wondering what had happened to Pat and who was caring for her. My father had desperately tried all channels to get me home on compassionate leave but failed. I felt so guilty that I had been really enjoying myself while this had been going on. Thankfully, at the same time as I received this news, there were further letters which said that Maisie had left the hospital and my father and mother had collected her and Pat and taken them home. She was progressing as well as could be expected.

I was now getting really bored doing nothing in Delhi, having seen and done everything worthwhile. I approached an officer and asked if he could do something to get me working again. He informed me that there was a vacancy for a signals officer at No 46 Staging Post, Jodhpur. I readily agreed to take it and was flown there on the first available plane. It turned out to be an excellent choice.

Jodhpur is in the middle of the Sind Desert, very hot indeed during the day, up to 120 degrees Fahrenheit, and quite chilly at nights. The airfield was a few miles away from the town of Jodhpur, governed by a Maharajah. He lived in a magnificent palace recently built, high up on the edge of a cliff, luxuriously elaborate and unbelievably large. While it was being built many workmen fell off the face of the cliff and were killed.

He was the Maharajah who was paid his weight in gold every year – and my God, he was fat. It seemed quite immoral that he should live in such opulence and splendour while his subjects were living barely above starvation level. And it appeared that the British Government ensured that his position was secure. The Prince of Wales had spent holidays here. Roaming the countryside were wild boars, and the Prince and his party would 'enjoy' themselves by 'pig-sticking'. How normal human beings can enjoy themselves by killing defenceless wild animals I shall never understand.

I soon settled down here. There were two units at this airfield, No 46 Staging Post and a Maintenance Unit which was much larger. Each unit had a Signals Officer, so I shared an office with my counterpart, a Scotsman, Mac. We got on very well together, visiting Hindu temples and other places of interest on our days off.

There are many wild dogs in India, called pi dogs. Some of them have become semi-domesticated by roaming the camp in search of food. I have always been a great dog-lover and able to communicate even with those dogs classified as dangerous. So I befriended a pi dog and each morning he would wait for me and follow me to the office. At morning break I would get my cup of tea and a wad (cake) and also buy sufficient of some food to provide a meal for my friend. Most of these pi dogs had blood-suckers on their back at just the point where they could neither scratch nor bite, which multiplied very rapidly. So one day I put a lighted cigarette so close to these insects that they just peeled off and he was free of them. Mac regarded my attachment to this dog with great disapproval, and he hated having him in the office with me.

Then came a very unfortunate incident. By mistake I locked the dog in the office one evening when I left. The next morning Mac opened up first. The office was in a complete shambles. Most likely because he had always lived in the open, the dog had panicked. He had jumped on the desk, scattered correspondence and files over the floor, pulled everything out of the cupboards and his footprints high up on the walls denoted what a frightened state he had been in. Mac was livid. He commandeered another office, moved out and that was the end of a beautiful friendship.

I also got great pleasure out of watching the habits of ants. I noticed there was a nest high up in the angled corner between the wall and ceiling. I would swat a fly and leave it on the desk or floor. A lone roaming ant would discover it. Being unable to move it himself, he would race off across the table, down the leg, across the floor and up the wall to the nest. Almost immediately an army of ants would emerge and follow the exact route back to the fly. They would carry it back to their nest although the last part was a vertical climb of eight feet. Ants must have quite a sophisticated method of communication. These diversions helped to pass the time away.

I had a lot of spare time, so when the post of Air Transit Officer became vacant I took it on as well. This necessitated supervising the loading of all aircraft, both military and those of TATA civilian airlines. By weighing passengers and their luggage I had to ensure that a plane was not overloaded. This often meant several people could not get aboard and then I would use a system of priorities to decide who would be able to travel. For those left behind I would often have to provide sleeping accommodation either on the camp or at the local hotel.

I also took on the job of Bar Officer, a post in which I had a keen personal interest. Official supplies of beer and spirits were unpredictable, but I had to ensure that there were always plenty to supply demand, so I would visit the town and ferret around to buy what was needed. Spirits were no problem, but beer was always in short supply.

Officers at Jodhpur were billeted in the old palace of the Maharajah, so our accommodation was very comfortable. There was a swimming pool, tennis court and squash court: almost a leisure centre hotel. There was also one 'bearer' (servant) allocated to each two officers. He made our beds, saw that we had clean clothes daily, ran our bath and generally made himself useful. A bearer was paid 120 rupees (£12) a month. They were all very smart, wore uniform clothes and were highly regarded by their fellow countrymen.

There was always plenty to do in the daytime, but after dinner there was little to pass the time away, so it was inevitable that I joined four others in a poker school. Naturally we drank while playing cards, and beer was almost unobtainable. Our card sessions took a long while, often lasting until the early hours of the morning. Each one would buy himself a bottle of gin or whisky and that bottle would be emptied by the time we finished playing. I drank gin, which I flavoured with the juice from limes which grew in abundance. I began to get bouts of indigestion, so I saw the Medical Officer. The conversation went as follows:

MD: 'What do you drink in the evening?'
Myself: 'Usually a bottle of gin.'
MD: 'Neat?'

Myself: 'No, I usually flavour it with the juice from
limes.'
MD: 'That's the problem, Lime juice is no good to
anybody. Top it up with water instead.'
So from then on my tipple was gin and water, and I
continued to drink a bottle every evening. I always slept
well.

At poker I won regularly and was classified as a 'lucky
bastard'. But it was not luck, it was mathematical skill in
being able to work out the odds for or against certain
combinations of cards and acting accordingly. I won a lot
of money. One evening a F/Lt finished the evening owing
me £200, for which he wrote me a cheque. I sent it home
to Maisie to bank. Two weeks afterwards Maisie wrote
saying it had been returned R/D. In the meantime the F/Lt
had been promoted to Squadron Leader, a senior officer. I
tackled him about it and he gave me ten post-dated
monthly cheques for £20 and they were all met. Our card
games were serious and we never let anyone off the hook.

This officer, however, was singularly unlucky on another
occasion. He suffered a recurrent attack of malaria, and
went into hospital. He had been in the RAF for many
years and contracted malaria periodically. When I visited
him he asked me if I would stand a bet he wanted to make
on the Derby and the Oaks, which were being run in
England the following week. I readily agreed and he made
a wager of 50 rupees (£5) on a horse in the Derby, 50
rupees on Midday Sun in the Oaks and a 50 rupee double.
And he handed me 150 rupees.

I visited him again a couple of evenings afterwards and
he told me he had been granted two weeks sick leave for

recuperation, that he was not very flush for money, so would I cancel his bet and return his cash, which I did. In due course both of his selections won, and he would have stood to draw about 1750 rupees. On this occasion I was a 'lucky bastard'.

Our CO of 46 Staging Post was S/Ldr Street, a man with a fine operational career on Bomber Command behind him, who had been awarded the Distinguished Flying Cross and bar, so naturally there was an affinity between us, as nearly all the other officers were non-operational ground staff. His great love in life was playing bridge, and being a CO he received invitations to play from many influential people. And always he would contact me and give me an order, 'You are playing bridge tonight, Mourton.' He never missed taking me as his partner, so I visited some of the most lavish homes. We always started with dinner, often a six course affair, so we ate and drank much more than was good for us, and then we would play until the early hours of the morning. Like many who had survived on Bomber Command, S/Ldr Street had a mad streak in him and our journeys back in his jeep were really hair-raising.

As Air Transit Officer I had a good relationship with TATA Airlines, a Company which ran civilian aircraft throughout India, and I received an invitation from the owner to his son's wedding. It was held on a wide expanse of lawn, lanterns dotted everywhere for illumination, tables laden with food, and an army of servants attending the guests of which there was a very large crowd. The remarkable thing was that when the feasting finished, the women retired to the house and were not seen again. The music started and the males were entertained by a large troupe of young dancing girls, who were also very proficient in other modes of entertainment. Apparently this was a Hindu tradition. It was a very enjoyable evening.

At Jodhpur we had a small contingent of Chinese operators and technicians, who were in contact with Chinese aircraft which were flying 'over the hump' (a range of high mountains) between India and China. I do not know for what purpose, but it was obviously to do with the fight against the mutual enemy, Japan. I became quite friendly with them. It so happened that I had to take a flight to Karachi to have teeth extracted (they were not filled in those days) and I was given a letter of introduction to some of their friends there.

It coincided with the Chinese New Year, so once again I was the guest at an unusual party. There were parades of evil, sinister looking dragons and animals; pageantry which I think was a display of fighting against wicked spirits; a wonderful firework display; and dancing routines performed by attractive slant-eyed Chinese maidens. Add to this plenty to eat and drink and a very enjoyable time was had until the early hours of the morning. After the party I was driven back to a large bungalow where my Chinese friends were living, and provided with a bed for the rest of the night.

In March 1945 I began flying again as a wireless operator on various Dakotas of Transport Command. This enabled me to visit many large towns in India and surrounding districts, often with stopovers which were most interesting and always in first class accommodation as we were officers. I visited Ceylon again and had three days in Ratmalana, but unfortunately it was not convenient to visit my brother.

Bombay was visited several times. On one occasion our crew visited Grant Road, which comprises only brothels, starting with a very high class establishment at one end, down to prostitutes in cages at the other end. Its reputation is well known by service men all over the world. We entered No 1, run then by Madame André, and only open to officers. There was no evidence of its actual purpose, and there was no obligation to indulge in the sexual activities. It resembled a good class club. There was a bar, music, tables and chairs, everything nicely decorated and in good taste. The drinks were very expensive, but one could dance with the hostesses without being propositioned. We spent an enjoyable evening, drinking very slowly: that's all. That is my story and I am sticking to it.

We visited all the main towns in India, and they differed from each other so much, as did the people, from being almost white in the far north to as black as the ace of spades in the south. These various journeys made the time pass very quickly.

Chapter Sixteen

I N JUNE I WAS given a totally different assignment. There existed a problem that aircraft were crashing and being lost when on long journeys during the monsoon season. Accordingly it was decided to open up emergency landing strips between airfields to which aircraft could divert when in difficulties. The first of these was scheduled to be laid out near a very small village, Narvai, which was south of Jaipur. I was sent in charge of twelve airmen to get the runway laid out and a W/T receiver and transmitter installed. We set off in a lorry with a supply of food (not very adequate), beds but no tents, various tools and the W/T equipment.

Following us was a bowzer full of drinking water, a supply of tablets to purify the water when we had to refill, and some barrels of petrol. We located the spot and it was obvious that a large amount of work was required to be done. There were hundreds of trees to be uprooted and the ground levelled. A contractor was commissioned to supply local labour for the heavy work.

Our stay here was most interesting. White people had rarely been seen, and it was quite usual to be followed by a dozen or so young black children, very curious and half scared. Turn round quickly, clap your hands, and they would turn tail and run for miles.

The only building we had was an open hut. After dark we lit an oil-lamp and congregated there singing songs and telling jokes to pass the time away, before going to bed in the open with a mosquito net over us. We had to put the legs of our beds into tins filled with paraffin to stop the insects crawling in with us.

One day we went out foraging and bought four chickens to supplement our diet. However, next morning four eggs were laid so we decided to defer the death sentence and instead to buy food to feed them with. We had them enclosed, but one night a pi dog got in and tore open the crop of one of the chickens before we could get to the rescue. One of our party was a hospital orderly in case of illness. He got out his sewing equipment, pushed the crop back in and then stitched it up. The chicken continued to lay.

One day one of the Indian workers had his leg cut very badly by an axe. Once again our hospital orderly did some sewing in a professional manner and this caused quite a sensation amongst the other workers. He was looked upon almost as a magician, and next morning when we awoke there was a line of patients with all kind of disabilities, skin complaints, blindness in grown-ups and little children. It was heart-rending as somehow we had to explain to them that he was unable to help them and they walked away disconsolately.

Eventually the runway was completed and the first plane to arrive was very welcome. It brought a further supply of food and more importantly our drink ration, two pints of beer for every man and for me two bottles of spirits. There had never been any distinction between myself and the airmen, apart from when things needed organising, so to emphasise our equality the drink was pooled between us. That evening we consumed the lot, our singing being much louder and our jokes bawdier.

The second plane was less welcome. About 10 am we were still sleeping off the effects of the previous evening when we were awakened by the noise of an aircraft circling overhead. We got up and lounged around with curiosity, waiting for it to land. I had not had a shave since we arrived, I was dressed only in a pair of shorts and probably showed the effect of my drinking ability the evening before.

When it landed and came to a halt a very high-ranking officer emerged and asked to speak to the officer in charge. He was the Air Officer Commanding the Group and had arrived from Delhi for an inspection. Very self-consciously I showed him around. He appeared quite pleased with the work we had done, and asked if there was anything we required that he could send along. Like a true commander he had accepted the situation as it was, and the circumstances we were working under. In general RAF officers were far more tolerant and less conscious of their rank than the other services.

Our lavatory was a well dug trench, about 4 feet by 3 feet and 2 feet deep with a pole across the middle for squatting on. Not very comfortable, but it served its purpose. We had no newspapers to read whilst sitting there, but there were interesting things to watch – 'shit beetles'. Two beetles, presumably male and female, would roll themselves a ball of excreta and then with one pushing and the other pulling would transport it up the side of the latrine and roll it along the sand until they found a suitable spot. Then they scratched away so that they and the ball disappeared into the sand. Presumably they mated and the ball provided food for their offspring.

Then there were many chameleons, so interesting to watch their colour change to match their environment, varieties of birds which we had never seen before and a profusion of insects. If anything died several vultures would appear from nowhere. I was told they hovered high in the sky with space between each one. Each one had its eyes on the ground below and also on the vulture on either side. When one dived to the ground the message was passed along the line to the others and eventually they all congregated on the dead animal, or one very near to death.

One day a small two-seater open cockpit aircraft arrived to take me back to headquarters to report, and then returned me to the landing strip. On both journeys we flew very low over the Taj Mahal, a very impressive sight.

One evening we took the lorry into Jaipur. There appeared to be no white people resident here and as a consequence the only facilities were for the locals, including once again prostitutes in cages, to be looked over by prospective customers. The speciality of the region is fancy metal work. I bought six egg cups in a tray. They were quite attractive, but we have never used them, and probably would not be able to find them now.

A local contractor had been erecting permanent

buildings, living quarters, housing for the W/T equipment and so on. They had almost been completed when the monsoon arrived and there is nothing quite like a monsoon. What have been dry, parched fields are suddenly covered by a foot of water, rivers start running again. But the main effect here was that the buildings suddenly disappeared – turned into a heap of rubble. Cement seemed to be unknown; a mixture of mud and gravel appeared to have been used.

And now, our work having almost finished, an aircraft arrived to take me back to Jodhpur. I had spent three unusual and interesting weeks. The twelve airmen and I had all got on so well together, even though conditions had been tough at times. I had worn only a pair of shorts throughout, always in the open, so I was almost as black as any native. I had to endure many ribald comments when I went back to the officers mess.

Once a year the Maharajah of Jodhpur invited the entire personnel of the airfield to his palace for the day. This comprised around 2,000 of us, and unbelievably we were not at all crowded. We had the run of the entire premises with the exception of the most interesting and intimate region, the apartments reserved for his harem. There were various competitions organised; the more energetic could play tennis or squash and there was a large swimming pool. There was an adequate and varied amount of food: sheep and pigs roasted whole on spits, various curries, chicken dishes etc. It was a very memorable day and we were all given a diary with a photograph of the Maharajah in full regalia in front.

Chapter Seventeen

AND THEN CAME a most unusual and momentous event. The whole camp mutinied, every single airman and NCO. The background to this should be examined. The war in Europe and the Far East had finished and there were great celebrations in England about which we heard and read but could not take part in, but for the average airman conditions were very hard in India. Temperatures soared to 120 degrees Fahrenheit and maintaining aircraft under these conditions was very difficult and uncomfortable. The quality of food had reached a very low level; the beer ration to which they were entitled was non-existent. There had been no diversions such as Ensa concerts, and they did not have the luxuries that officers enjoyed. And many had been here for three or four years. It was common knowledge that troops were being demobilised in England and other theatres of war. Prisoners of war of the Japanese were being given priority from the Far East, and very deservedly so. Lack of transport was causing undue delay for repatriation from India, but no information or explanation about this was given by the authorities.

One day as Duty Officer I visited the dining hall after a meal, with the usual enquiry, 'Any complaints?' There was immediately an ear-splitting noise of plates being banged on tables, and abuse being shouted concerning the food. I made a report concerning this, but apparently, as with other reports and entreaties, it had been disregarded by the people who should have endeavoured to put right these grievances.

The mutiny itself was well organised. Meetings had been held and speeches made in hangars in complete darkness so that the ringleaders would be difficult to identify. It all began on a pre-arranged morning. The Station Commander went down to take the parade at 6.30 am as usual, but not a single person had arrived. He was confused, was his watch wrong? was it Sunday? He returned to the officers mess to make enquiries. Then he realised the truth; and by a strange coincidence we had had one hell of a party the evening before in the officers mess, the piano had been overturned and it was in a state of chaos. Then he made a mistake; he assumed the officers were also involved, and he put under arrest the most senior officer who had been present in the mess the preceding evening, a squadron leader. Then he made another mistake: he called in the Indian Army. They arrived in full force in armoured cars, guns at the ready, and looking trigger happy and ready to have a go at the slightest excuse. All work ceased on the camp for several days.

The outcome was that a delegation arrived from Group Headquarters including the Air Officer Commanding to conduct an enquiry. Representatives were invited from the airmen, not necessarily the ones who had organised the mutiny. Probably there has never been a more harmonious ending to such a happening. From that time on the food improved, the beer ration arrived on time and the first Ensa concert entertained us shortly afterwards. I think the Station Commander was posted away elsewhere and nobody received any punishment. And so life returned to normal at Jodhpur, but one could sense a much better spirit and atmosphere.

These events showed me that a body of men, acting in unison with no dissidents, with a firm resolve, can attain almost anything within reason. There had been many previous mutinies in the services over the years which had ended in disaster simply because a percentage of the men had opted not to take part, enabling the more urgent work to be carried out, and the death penalty had been carried out on those assumed to be the ringleaders.

The remarkable thing is that this mutiny was kept completely secret. No news appeared about it at all in England. But the news spread to other stations in India, and apparently the mutiny spread right across the Continent. It was some time after the end of the war that a question was asked in the House of Commons and the minimum of information was given in reply. Recently however a programme appeared on TV called 'Secret Happenings' or some similar title, which dealt with the mutiny in great detail. I was interviewed in the first instance at home, and then I travelled to London for an appearance before the cameras and mikes. Later the programme was broadcast. It is a peculiar sensation to see yourself appearing, looking somewhat different to how you imagined you were.

We had received earlier the news about that most devastating raid, the dropping of the atom bomb on Hiroshima on 6 August. At that time we could not comprehend what exactly had happened; conventional bombs were the sole extent of our knowledge. Gradually information filtered through concerning the secret work that had been going on for years to produce such a weapon of mass destruction. It turned out that Hitler had authorised similar experiments, and we were extremely lucky that he was defeated before they were completed. Then followed a further atom bomb being dropped on Nagasaki on 9 August. The atom bomb had the destructive power of 200,000 tons of TNT. The first one killed an estimated 130,000 persons, with many more dying later from burns and radiation. There will always be a debate about whether the second bomb was necessary or merely the continuation of experiments to satisfy the curiosity of the military chiefs. Certainly reports suggest that Japan was already suing for peace.

With the dropping of the two atomic bombs on Japan, the enemy was suing for peace and it was obvious that the war was nearly at an end. Group Captain Cheshire, ex 102 Squadron (his career has been dealt with in earlier pages) flew with the Americans as the official British observer at these new deadly weapons. The armistice was finally signed on 2 September on board the US battleship *Missouri*, anchored in Tokyo Bay. It was a foregone conclusion and certainly was not celebrated much at Jodhpur. We were all more concerned about when we would return home.

Demobilisation was a massive operation, needing a high

degree of organisation. Every serviceman had a demob number which depended on age and length of service. As I had enlisted right at the beginning I had the lowest possible number for my age, 13. Demobilisation began with those people numbered 1 and gradually rose upwards, but each trade or profession was treated differently according to supply and demand. I was very hopeful of an early demob; but unfortunately Signals Officers were most needed and were lagging behind in the demob race. Also, as previously mentioned, lack of transport caused serious delay for troops in India.

About the middle of November I was disappointed to receive a posting to Bangkok in Siam (now renamed Thailand) which was definitely in the wrong direction. So I was flown to Calcutta to wait for embarkation to Siam. The district of Calcutta was in the middle of one of its worst droughts in its history. Scores were lying dead from hunger in the roads, and dustbins were being raked over for any sign of food. I was accommodated in a large five star hotel, where everyone was being served with large multi-course meals, far too much for anyone to eat, except the most gluttonous. It seemed so immoral for a comparative few to be enjoying far more than they needed, while the multitudes were starving. And yet nobody seemed to care.

After one or two days I visited an orderly room to draw some money. Quite by chance I happened to read a communication on the notice board. To my great surprise I saw Signals Officers Group 13 were being repatriated. I had a choice: I could ignore the information and proceed to Bangkok, a town which in those days seemed mysterious and exciting, or I could proceed home. Naturally I chose the latter, so I arranged a railway warrant to go to Bombay and left immediately. Bangkok probably coped quite well minus one Signals Officer. It was a long journey to Bombay, but as an officer very comfortable. We were *burra sahibs* (big chiefs). When a train stopped at a station at a meal time, all the privileged would disembark and proceed to a restaurant, and the train would not carry on until the last one returned, no matter how long he took. Sometimes it must have made the timetable look a little inaccurate.

On arrival at Bombay I went into a transit mess. We were all champing at the bit to be loaded onto a boat for Blighty. I spent several days watching a Test Match and visited the racecourse twice, so there was plenty to occupy my time. I also bought some Eastern carpets from a warehouse, guaranteed to be delivered to my home within two months. They must have been delayed somewhere, because fifty years later they still have not been delivered. A confidence trick? I do not know. They could have been stolen anywhere on the way. Then eventually I received instructions to board a troopship, and soon we weighed anchor.

Our first stop was at Aden. The only people to disembark were taken off by tender. These were those unfortunates who had indulged in the delights of the brothels and contracted VD but the symptoms had not been apparent until they were on their way home. They had to endure ribald remarks from the crowds lining the decks.

As usual I found myself participating in a game of

bridge. We kept the same partners from Bombay to Liverpool, a journey which took four weeks. We played several hours every day, but we also partook of a fair amount of exercise by running round the decks, attending gym classes etc. There were other sights to interest us: Arabs flashing their weapons on the banks of the Suez Canal, much to our envy; flying fish in the Mediterranean; and some very heavy storms in the Bay of Biscay. The weather gradually got colder and finally we arrived in Liverpool on 10 December.

Chapter Eighteen

ARRIVING BACK IN England, we were given a very quick medical examination, although anyone who had visited the brothels in Bombay could subject himself to more rigorous tests. Not for us psychiatrists, and counsellors hadn't been invented.

We were then kitted out with civilian clothes. As I remember, it was a suit, a trilby hat, socks, underwear and a pair of boots or shoes. We were allowed two weeks disembarkation leave, but we didn't have to report back, it was the end of our service. One felt rather strange after over six years of service life in uniform.

I received a railway warrant to London, and telephoned Maisie with my time of arrival so she could meet me. Naturally I was tremendously excited, looking forward to meeting my wife and my little girl whom I had not seen for so long. We met on the railway platform with a very loving and passionate embrace. I can still see my little Pat looking up at me very curiously, with thick blond hair, wearing a nice blouse and tartan skirt. She was very pretty. But she treated me with great reserve, and needed a lot of persuading before she would kiss me. She had been four years old the previous September.

Fortunately, while I was in India, Maisie had bought a house in Addiscombe, a suburb of Croydon. It is interesting to compare the situation at the end of 1945 with the conditions existing today. It cost £950 and the deposit was £25; the mortgage rate was 4 per cent and had been for decades. Repayments worked out around £1 a week, when the average weekly wage was £5. So a man could buy a good house for 20 per cent of his wages; no need for his wife to go to work to pay off the mortgage. Our house was a three-bedroom semi-detached with a separate garage and a nice garden, in one of the more expensive districts. When we arrived there Maisie showed me proudly around. She had bought it on her own initiative, with a little help from my father. She had also attended auction sales and answered advertisements to buy second-hand furniture at the very low prices that were all we could afford. I considered myself very lucky to fall into such an ideal ready-made home.

Pat was still regarding me as a stranger and that night she really hated me. She had been sleeping in the same bed with Maisie and now this strange man had entered her life, had usurped her position next to her Mum, while she had been banished to a separate bedroom. One can understand why she did not regard me in a very favourable light. But I always had a way with children; I told her stories and played games with her and we were very soon a happy family. Fortunately, I had made my homecoming just before Christmas, with all the preparations and expectations that please children so much.

Civilian life required some adjustment. Instead of moving around I was anchored. I had left many very good friends and companions, and I was now in a strange district with my pre-war friends scattered far and wide or dead. I now had to think for myself, the first time for many years. But soon it all worked out. So ended just over six years in the RAF since I had joined in 1939. Very few indeed of that intake had survived. Looking back I realised how lucky I had been. I had missed the posting at Yatesbury on to Blenheims, completed a tour of operations on Whitleys, a few on Wellingtons and quite a long period at OTUs. The posting to India had probably been a blessing in disguise.

In 1940, with Maisie seriously ill and having a kidney removed, and myself at the start of a career as a wireless operator/air gunner on bombers, I wonder what odds a bookmaker would have given against us both being fit and well sixty years later at the age of eighty-three years: 50-1? 200-1? When the war ended statistics showed that out of every 100 aircrew who joined Bomber Command in 1939, 78 had been killed, 12 were prisoners-of-war and 10 were alive in England, and of the 22 that actually survived many had physical or mental disabilities, some of which appeared later.

But in general, airmen nearly always had a bed to sleep on and reasonable food to eat. We didn't suffer the privations, dirt and disease that were the lot for years of the armies fighting in Burma and the Far East in general. Those who suffered most of all were the POWs in Japanese hands. Disease and hunger killed almost half of them. Those who returned to England were in a pitiful state of health, most weighing only 5 or 6 stone. But none of them received a just reward.

Once in civvy street I realised my hearing was impaired owing to the noise experienced in the old aircraft, and I had a heart condition, possibly due to the hypertension experienced when flying over hostile country. I was duly examined by specialists, pronounced 30 per cent disabled and awarded a pension. This increases every year in line with inflation and has now reached the sum of £31 a week, not very much considering the difficulty and embarrassment it has often caused me. The heart condition necessitated taking Digoxin tablets for thirty years until I had a pacemaker fitted.

But now loomed the prospect of becoming employed. I had left school at the age of sixteen years, having matriculated with honours. I took up work in an accountant's office and also a shipping office, but both proved dead-end jobs. Then a vacancy had become available in the company for which my father worked, and I decided to take it. This was S.M. Bryde and Co Ltd., Brixton, and I was required to take orders over the telephone and deal with customers on the trade counter, and generally make myself useful. It was a company wholesaling wallpaper and paints to decorators and the few retail shops that existed. My home was about four miles away, which distance I cycled, and even returned for a meal during my dinner hour break.

Sometime later in 1934, Mr Whitely, the managing director, came on a periodic visit from head office. I had acquired a driving licence (there was no test then), and I was asked to drive him to Shand Kydd, a wallpaper mill, to buy clearances. We had dinner at The Plough, Clapham on the way back, and I took the opportunity to ask him if I could be a 'Commercial Traveller' (this was always the term used for representatives). He was against the idea at first, because of my age, but under pressure agreed that when I cleared up my work in the office I could call on new accounts only.

Very few representatives had cars, most used public transport, which was very time consuming and a few still used a pony and trap in country districts. However, I decided to use my bicycle. A sturdy carrier on the back held two large cases, containing pattern books and samples of brushes and sidelines. On top was a bowler hat. My procedure was to park round a corner, take off my cycle clips, put on my bowler hat, pick up my two bags and make the call. So, at 7.00 am on a summer's morning, at the age of eighteen, I had commenced my career. By 8.00 am I had opened three accounts with small orders from decorators who commenced work at 7.00 am. I was jubilant. My wage was £3 a week, plus a small commission which usually averaged £1.

It was hard work, especially when I cycled in the rain, wearing waterproof jacket and leggings. Often too, there would be up to 8 miles or so between calls. I usually started out at 7.00 am and finished at 8.00 pm in the evening, due to the fact that many customers were decorators who did not arrive back home until the evening. Often I would be entertained to an evening meal with the family.

A commercial traveller always wore a hat. He carried a silver cigarette case and, after shaking hands, he would offer his customer a cigarette – this was almost a ritual. If the customer lit up, he would do likewise. Never was a customer referred to by his christian name, and in correspondence he would be addressed as A. Brown Esq.

My first big break came completely by surprise. I called for the first time on a large property company, T.W. & H. Sloman in Camberwell. I had an offer, 30 'Specials'; clearances which had just been brought from Shand Kydd at 3½d. a roll to sell at 6d. The buyer ordered 240 rolls throughout, amounting to over £100. I pedalled my hardest back to Brixton with this order, the biggest I had seen anyone take. I received a letter of commendation from Mr Whiteley and was made a full time commercial traveller. A few months later I had saved enough to buy a 1929 Austin 7 for £25 and I was now really in business. I repped for five years, quite successfully, until war was declared.

So when I was demobbed my father and I decided to set up on our own as a decorator's merchant. We took a small shop in Croydon, and we were joined a few months later by my brother on being released from the navy. The rent was £250 a year, including a nice upstairs flat.

In 1946 supplies were very short and allocated on pre-war turnover, so we did not qualify. But then emerged two pieces of luck. I heard that a new wallpaper mill was starting up, Graham and Brown, so I immediately proceeded to Blackburn and met Henry Brown. He had just been demobbed from the army; we had a lot in common, and a close friendship started which lasted until he died a few years ago. I called on him every month and always obtained a good supply. At this time wallpaper was like gold dust. As an example, several times we bought brown lining in reels, had it embossed, cut into

rolls and bundled. It was sold out as wallpaper with no
difficulty.

The second piece of luck was that I contacted a Bomber
Command acquaintance who now had a good position
with Goodlass Wall. He gave me an allocation of fifty
gallons of Combinol a month. Paint could only be
supplied to decorators who had permits issued by the local
council for War Damage Repairs. These permits were then
sent to a paint manufacturer for replacement, but only the
permit number had to be quoted, so quite illegally we
would send the permit number to more than one
manufacturer. This gave us additional stock which we
could sell 'off the ration'.

We all worked long and hard. In 1949 wallpaper became
more plentiful and we were now buying from several other
mills. We issued our first pattern book, Mouratone, at the
end of 1949 and distributed it to decorators and the many
wallpaper shops that were now opening up. It was
an immediate success. We also started to open retail
shops and by 1953 trade was really buoyant. We were
approached by a large company who wanted to buy us out
for £39,000. I had just moved into a four-bedroomed
house in Croydon at a cost of £3,000. My father was
desperate to sell out, but my brother and I were against it.
We were equal partners, but my father had provided the
small initial capital. I decided to take a desperate chance. I
approached Midland Bank for an overdraft of £13,000 to
pay my father out. I had no security to offer but they
agreed and my father retired.

I was doing all the repping and my brother supervised
the office and warehouse. We paid our staff well over the

going rate, and also distributed a bonus at every year-end. This paid off; no one ever left and we had no difficulty in recruiting staff as we continued to expand. We did our job well and without actually trying, we found ourselves to be the biggest independent wholesaler by the 1960s. We were selling four million rolls a year.

By 1972 we possessed two large freehold warehouses and fifty-five shops, many of which were freehold. It had all been financed out of profits; we owed no money and had a large bank balance. We were employing around two hundred staff.

Then, at least for me, disaster struck. In July 1972 we received a phone call from Grimshawe Holdings (a public company owning many other merchants, garages, etc.) asking if they could have a discussion with us with a view to purchasing our companies. I wanted to turn it down, but my brother persuaded me to meet them. After much discussion they offered us nine times our net profit for 1972. I was very happy running our own operation; I had no real wish to obtain a large sum of money. I resisted the offer as much as possible, but finally had to give in because of the advice given by our accountants and solicitors and because many of our staff thought they would have more security as part of a large public company.

Our net profit for 1972 amounted to £205,000, so Grimshawe's offer was £1,840,000, to be divided between my brother and myself. We had the option to take shares at 35p, when they were quoted at 42p on the stock exchange, or cash. They offered me a very acceptable five-year contract and because of this I took it nearly all in shares, taking only £90,000 in cash. I gave £5,000 each to my four daughters and £5,000 each to four charities and I bought a Mercedes, my reasoning being that when I wanted more money, I could sell some shares. Having been a socialist all my life and realising my staff had contributed as much as me to our success, I gave away nearly half my shares to them. The professional advice I was given was that I could give up to the value of £1,000 to any one person without incurring Capital Gains Tax. Those who qualified for £4,000, for instance, had their shares split between husband, wife, children, etc.

In January 1973, having completed the deal, my wife and I left for a month's holiday in Australia to visit our daughter. When we left, the shares had been quoted at 43p; when we returned, they had dropped to 25p and they were difficult to sell. They continued to drift downwards. Grimshawe himself resigned, owing a large sum of money to the company. Apparently, a fictitious profit had been shown on the balance sheet for 1972, which came to light at the end of 1973. There was also an overdraft of £3,000,000.

The shares eventually fell to $1/2$p and then I heard no more. I had lost the lot.

But even worse was to follow. The Inland Revenue contacted me in 1979, and enquired what I had done with the balance of my shares in 1972. I told them I had given them to the staff. They replied that gifting shares was the same as selling them and I was subject to Capital Gains Tax on them. The advice I had been given was completely wrong. Somebody phoned me from Edinburgh and made an appointment to see me at the Inland Revenue office in

Crawley, as he was flying down to Gatwick. I went along with my accountant to meet him on a Wednesday at 11.00 am. We both sat at a desk facing him. He outlined the tax involved (the shares being worth about 40p when I gave them away), plus 9% interest to 1979, plus £10,000 penalty for not divulging what I had done. It amounted to £144,000 to be paid within thirty days and I had almost nothing. I became overcome with frustration, anger and the unfairness of it all. Sitting there in front of him I had a heart attack, and was rushed to Crawley Intensive Care Unit. I was there for just over a week and then convalesced for two weeks. I had a pacemaker fitted, which completely improved my health.

The Inland Revenue still wanted their money but were content to wait a little longer for it. My mother died soon afterwards and I received £58,000 from the sale of the house I owned in which she lived. I sold the leases on two shops I had acquired, for £20,000. This money and everything I made subsequently went straight to the Inland Revenue. I finished paying in 1989. My generosity to my staff had been very costly, but it grieved me that they had also lost out; their nest eggs had disappeared.

When I came out of Crawley Hospital in 1979 I started up again, having the goodwill of customers and suppliers. The company is still going strong but with a smaller staff who are dedicated and loyal. I still get a thrill when I book a big order and realise I am 'in the swim'. I travel regularly to Eire, France and Belgium; my wife always accompanies me and enjoys as much as I do meeting customers, entertaining them to dinner and listening to the news on the grapevine. Not really hard work.

After eleven years my original pacemaker was removed and a new one fitted, a very lengthy job because flesh had grown round and was adhering to it. The operation took two hours with only a local injection. However one year afterwards when I went for a routine check up, I was informed that the pacemaker fitted was one of a faulty batch and might cease to function at any time, so I was provided with a third one. They are a marvellous invention, giving you a new lease of life. I play tennis twice a week, table tennis with my wife every evening, and usually walk ten miles every week-end. I think everyone should have one fitted.

Life teaches us many lessons. It taught me that large sums of money do not bring happiness. It is far more valuable to have a loving partner (we have been married fifty-nine years), to be part of a loving, happy family, to have good health and genuine friends and enough money to rub along on – in that order.

I would be no happier than I am now, however much money I had. I am still in good health at the age of eighty-three years.

Douglas and Maisie, 104 Squadron Reunion 1997.

Chapter Nineteen

WHEN I WAS demobbed my main concern was to put my war service in the past and to get on with the future. I didn't apply for the medals for which I had qualified. My grandchildren on several occasions asked me to claim them; I promised I would and then forgot all about it.

One day at a family gathering one of my grandchildren asked me if I remembered my service number. 'Yes,' I replied, '904638.' About a month later I was handed a small heavy package. On opening it I found the five medals for which I had qualified.

Apparently she had written to the Air Ministry, giving the illusion that I had died, without actually saying so. They had sent her the medals and also the complete details of my service history.

So now on formal occasions I am able to display very proudly my campaign medals.

Chapter Twenty

Almost an Obituary

MAISIE AND I went on our usual holiday to Australia on 8 December 1998. Just before we left at the end of February my daughter said that for a birthday present she had arranged a trip in a Tiger Moth for me at Janderkot airport with the Royal Aero Club. This was the type of aircraft I had flown in 1937.

During my war service the narrow escapes I survived and the amount of money I won at poker had earned me the title of Lucky Doug (and sometimes Lucky Bastard).

I was introduced to the pilot and informed him that I had flown Tiger Moths over sixty ears ago and I had been proficient then in aerobatics. On learning my history the pilot agreed to perform those same aerobatics, so during the hour's flight we looped the loop, rolled, spun and flew upside down. But youth had given way to old (?) age. I found the experience traumatic and frightening and the aircraft seemed so fragile after travelling in jumbo jets.

On landing I told my daughter untruthfully that I had enjoyed the flight enormously, so she suggested I had another flight the next day, and the pilot said if so I could

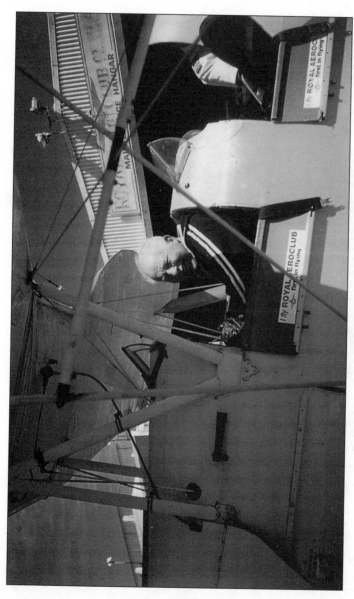

Douglas at controls of Tiger Moth, February 1998.

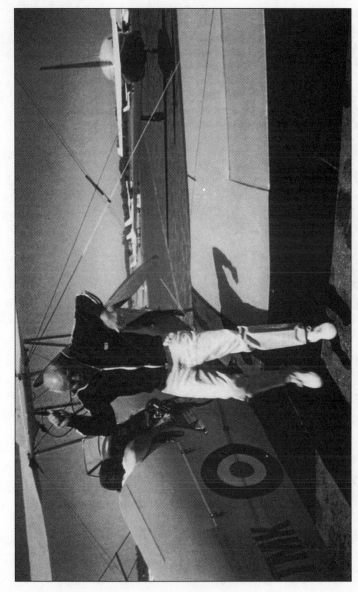

Alighting after flight in Tiger Moth, February 1998.

take over. I turned down the offer, saying I had packing to do (the only thing I pack is a bottle of whisky).

Arriving back in England I found the enclosed fax from my daughter. Yes, it was the same aircraft that I had flown in the previous day. Probably it was the very next flight. What a good job I never accepted the offer of a second flight.

But the biggest piece of luck I had was when I met Maisie accidentally in a pub. Next Christmas Day we celebrate our Diamond Wedding anniversary, sixty years of happiness.

DEAR DAD.

" LUCKY DOUG STRIKES AGAIN "

LOVE PAT

Tiger Moth death loop

By BRUCE BUTLER and INGRID JACOBSON

THE pilot and passenger of a Tiger Moth biplane died yesterday when the aircraft disintegrated.

Witnesses said parts of the plane tore off as the Tiger Moth came out of a loop.

It plummeted to the ground and exploded about 1.30pm in semi-rural Mundijong, about 56km south of Perth.

It is believed the plane crashed close to a farmhouse.

The alarm was raised by the owners and Wellard man Dave Whiting, who watched it spiral into the ground.

The property owner said he was inside his house, heard a bang and saw the fire, then realised it was a plane crash.

"First thing we knew was we heard a bang. We went outside and saw the smoke and flames," he said.

"Then we realised it was a plane — we're lucky it didn't hit the house."

The Tiger Moth was destroyed and the crash caused a small grass fire.

The Fire Brigade and St John Ambulance rushed to the scene. It is believed the pilot and his male passenger were killed on impact and incinerated.

Tiger Moths regularly fly over the city on joy flights from Jandakot.

The plane took off

from Jandakot, but the Royal Aero Club was unable to confirm last night if the plane was one of theirs.

Mr Whiting, 51, a refinery process operator of Thorne Place, Wellard about 10km from the crash site, was outside his house when he saw the Tiger Moth spiral in the ground.

I didn't think any

body could survive that," a shocked Mr Whiting said.

"We were watching it do the loop but when it came out of it, it appeared that some parts came off it.

"The wings didn't actually come off but it looked like someone was throwing something out of the plane.

It was like the wings

which support the wings pull apart way. The wings were straight up as the plane was coming down.

"It just dived/down and spiralled into the ground like a corkscrew.

It went straight into a dive and we watched the pieces coming down for quite a while after the plane. It was bright yellow

It didn't appear to be

engine failure. We could hear the engine revving during the loop and we only heard it stop when the plane crashed out of sight

"Then we saw some smoke.

Bureau of Air Safety investigators were at the scene last night.

Police who have identified the pilot did not release his name

□ Only the burnt, metal backbone remains of this Tiger Moth that crashed killing two people